THE GREAT
FISH
— AND —
SEAFOOD
COOKBOOK

Introduced by Beverley Piper
Recipes compiled by Judith Ferguson
Photographed by Peter Barry
Edited by Jillian Stewart
Designed by Claire Leighton

5033 The Great Fish and Seafood Cookbook
This edition published 1997 by CLB
Distributed in the USA by BHB International Inc.,
30 Edison Drive, Wayne, New Jersey 07470
© 1992 CLB International, Godalming, Surrey, UK
All rights reserved
Printed and bound in Singapore
ISBN 1-85833-750-X

THE GREAT
FISH
—AND—
SEAFOOD
COOKBOOK

JUDITH FERGUSON

CLB

CONTENTS

INTRODUCTION

Americans adore seafood, and are eating more and more of it every year. Seafood evokes memories of shrimping, crabbing and watching fishermen return with their catches. It is these happy memories which contribute to many people's love of seafood. What other valuable food is available in such variety?

Nothing tastes quite like fresh seafood, it is naturally tender and will only toughen if overcooked. There is such a tremendous variety of seafood available that it makes sense to learn more about this crucial source of nutrients and how it can best be incorporated into a diet which will please the whole family.

Fish is a wonderful food which is high in body building proteins and low in calories. White fish contains practically no fat, whilst oily fish varies in fat content from 0.5% - 20% and contains the sort of fatty acids which doctors believe may actually assist in preventing coronary heart disease.

Fish also contains almost no carbohydrate and is an excellent source of vitamins, and oily fish is particularly high in the fat soluble vitamins A and D, thiamin and riboflavin.

With all these important benefits to boast of, it is obvious why more use should be made of this easy-to-obtain food which is both delicious and nutritious. Sadly, many people have misconceptions about fish and shellfish, believing it is difficult to prepare and cook. This is just not true, follow the instructions given in the following pages and the different methods of preparing and cooking will become surprisingly simple.

One of the most common complaints about fish is that it smells. A famous chef once said "Fish should smell like the tide. Once they smell like fish, it's too late." So make sure when you buy fish that it has a wonderful "straight from the shore" aroma and is moist and fresh.

CHOOSING FISH

This selection of popular shellfish (left) includes: a hard-shell crab (top left); a cooked lobster (top right); oysters, which can be purchased in the shell or shucked (second row, left); a soft shell or blue crab is one which sheds its shell (second row, middle); mussels are purchased in the shell; scallops (third row, left) are freshest when purchased in the shell; clams (third row middle) can be puchased with or without their shells; prawns can be bought in many different ways, uncooked (third row, right), cooked, without heads and whole; squid (bottom right) can be bought fresh or frozen.

Fish is often classified in different ways - firstly according to the type of flesh:-

White Fish has a distinctive white flesh and includes such favorites as cod, sole and sea bass.

Oily Fish has oil distributed through its flesh, giving it a gray or red tinge. This group includes trout, mackerel and sardines.

Shellfish is the group enclosed in a shell and is further classified into two groups - crustaceans usually have limbs and a shell, such as crabs and lobster, whilst

molluscs e.g.. mussels, oysters etc. have a shell only.

Fish are also classified into groups determined by their shape:-

Round Fish have a rounded body with eyes at either side of the head and always swim dorsal fin up. This a very large group which includes a whole range of fish from freshwater salmon to sharks.

Flat Fish have both eyes on the top of their head, they swim on their sides, and are quick and easy to cook. This group includes skate and flounder.

Fish can be bought in a whole manner of shapes, sizes and cuts. Above is a small selection including clockwise: a whole flat fish, a cleaned round fish, a cleaned fish with head and tail removed, a fish steak, chunks of white fish, an unskinned butterflied steak, skinned fillets, unskinned fillets, and a whole round fish.

Buying Fish

When selecting fresh fish for the table it is important to choose the freshest fish possible. It is advantageous to buy a whole fish as it is very often cheaper than prepared cuts and is easier to judge for freshness. It should look moist and fresh, the eyes should be bright, the flesh firm, the gills red, the scales should sparkle and there should definitely be no unpleasant odor! Some fish have a natural slime which is easily removed by rinsing so don't be put off by it. If it is not possible or desirable to buy a whole fish, use the same guidelines when you select fish fillets or steaks. The flesh should look moist, bright, and white fish should be really white.

If possible fish should be used on the day of purchase, but if it must be stored it should be cleaned, washed and kept in the refrigerator overnight in a sealed container. Shellfish deteriorate rapidly and should always be bought for immediate use.

You will find a wide variety of fish and seafood at your local fish market, all of which you can buy ready prepared or whole. Cleaning and preparing fish is not at all difficult, just follow the step-by-step photographs and you will be surprised at how quickly you can have your fish ready for cooking.

Frozen Fish

Fresh fish is seasonal but frozen fish is, of course, available all year round. It is an excellent way to buy fish as only the very best quality fish is frozen and it is frozen as soon as it is caught to preserve the freshness. Frozen fish is almost always prepared for cooking before freezing, making it particularly easy for the cook to handle.

White fish may be stored in a domestic freezer for up to four months, whereas oily fish, because of its high fat content, is best consumed within three months. Shellfish, particularly shrimp, should be consumed within two months of being frozen. Home-made fish dishes also freeze well, but should also not be stored for longer than two months. For the best results defrost frozen fish overnight in the refrigerator.

Canned Fish

Canned fish is a wonderful store cupboard standby which keeps fresh more or less indefinitely and is therefore valuable for outdoor enthusiasts and the like, as well as for convenience meals when unexpected guests arrive. Oily fish is particularly suitable for canning and is useful in a large number of recipes.

Smoked Fish

Smoking is a method of preserving fish which results in its characteristic "smoky" flavor – kippers is probably one of the best known smoked fish available, however smoked mackerel is also becoming more widely available and is often served as a appetizer. Becoming ever more popular is smoked salmon, which is prepared by cleaning and filleting the fresh fish, then smoking the fillets in a cold smoker often over apple chips and oak sawdust. The resulting smoked salmon has a strong color, translucent appearance and tastes wonderful!

Food Value Fish

Nutritionally speaking, fish is one of the most valuable foods available to man. It is an excellent source of protein, which is needed for the growth and repair of body cells. It is also low in carbohydrates and saturated fats. Oily fish is rich in the fat-soluble vitamins A and D and all fish is rich in thiamin, riboflavin, niacin, B6, B12 pantothenic acid and biotin. Fish is also an excellent source of minerals, which are vitally necessary for the body's growth and functioning. Some of the smaller varieties of fish which are eaten whole, bones and all, provide a useful amount of calcium.

Fish is also fairly low in calories, especially when compared with other valuable protein foods such as meat and cheese. The approximate calorie counts below indicate just how useful fish is in a healthful diet:-

1oz of cod, steamed or poached in water	24 calories
1oz raw, ground beef	55 calories
1oz of leg of pork	72 calories
1oz Cheddar cheese	102 calories
1oz tuna in brine, canned	32 calories

Fish is quite rightly making a comeback – it is readily available, fairly cheap and very versatile. The versatility of fish extends to the ways in which it may be cooked, so try the following methods, always remembering never to overcook.

PREPARING FISH AND SEAFOOD

HOW TO SCALE AND FIN A ROUND FISH

1

Holding the fish firmly by the tail, scrape towards the head of the fish with a scaler or the blunt side of a knife.

2

Rinse the fish thoroughly under cold running water to remove any remaining scales and residue which may be clinging to the skin.

3

Trim the dorsal fin with a pair of scissors. To remove the whole fin, snip through most of the fin in the direction of the head and then pull.

CLEANING A ROUND FISH

1

Holding the body of the fish firmly, cut the head off just behind the gills. The head may be saved for use in fish stock or soup.

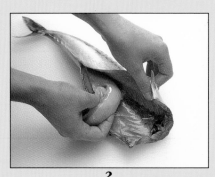

2

Cut down the underside of the fish to the tail and remove the innards, which should come out with ease.

3

Clean and remove any remaining residue by rinsing the fish thoroughly in cold running water.

FILLETING A ROUND FISH

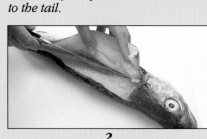

1

Holding the fish firmly, cut along the backbone from just behind the head to the tail.

2

Cut across the fish and slide the knife between the ribs and the flesh.

3

Carefully lift the fillet away, taking care not to break up the flesh.

SKINNING A FLAT FISH

Dip your fingers in salt to get a good grip then hold the fish by its tail and make a cut across the skin just above the tail.

Begin peeling the skin away from the cut. Pull the skin over the head, turn the fish over and pull the skin off of the underside.

1   **2**

SKINNING A FILLET

1

Get a firm grip on the tail end of the fillet, make a cut across the flesh and ease the fillet away from the skin in a sliding motion.

FILLETING A FLAT FISH

1

After skinning the fish, cut down, but not through, the backbone from behind the head to the tail.

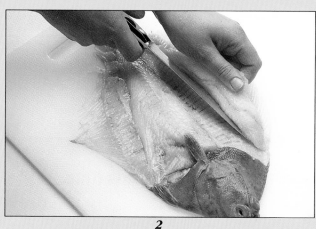

2

Insert the knife under the flesh at the top of the fish and cut down between the flesh and the bones until the fillet lifts off. Repeat on the other side.

OPENING OYSTERS

1

2

Hold the oyster tightly in one hand, and with the other, insert the oyster knife into the hinge, twisting until the shell opens.

Slide the blade under the oyster and cut through the connecting muscle to separate the oyster from its shell.

PREPARING MUSSELS

1 Scrub the mussels to remove any sand or barnacles.

Debeard the mussels by pulling the byssus which protrudes from the shell.

2

REMOVING MEAT FROM HARD-SHELL CRAB

1

Hold the crab firmly, twist apron flap and gently pull, removing the intestinal vein which is attached to the apron.

4

Crack the crab in two and remove any meat left on the central body section.

6

Scoop out the soft brown meat from the crab shell.

2

Holding the crab firmly with one hand, gently prise the shell off and put to one side for later use.

3

Remove the gills or "dead men's fingers" and discard.

5

Crack open the legs and extract the leg meat with a crab pick.

7

If using the shell to serve the meat, break of the rough edges and cut to form a neat edge.

8

The crab meat is now ready to be used in a recipe or can be served in the shell.

PREPARING LOBSTER

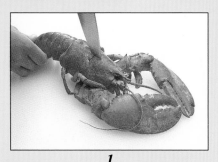

1

Using a sharp knife, cut the lobster down the center, beginning behind the head.

2

Cut right through the lobster from head to tail to separate in two.

3

Remove the tomalley (green liver) from the lobster.

PREPARING SHRIMP

1

Remove the legs of the shrimp and break off the shell by bending both sides backwards.

2

Cut down the back of the shrimp, cutting deep enough just to expose the intestinal vein which should then be removed.

PREPARING SQUID

1

Detach the tentacles and hard beak from the body of the squid by holding the tentacles and pulling gently.

4

Holding the body of the lobster, break the tail section away from the body.

5

Break the tail section apart and remove the meat.

6

Cut the large part of the claw away from the bits which do not contain any meat.

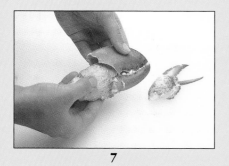

7

Crack the claws open to remove the meat.

8

The easiest way to remove the meat from the claws is with your fingers.

9

The meat from the shells should come out in one piece.

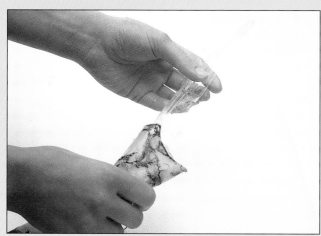

2

Remove the transparent quill and any remaining entrails by running your fingers along the body to the open end.

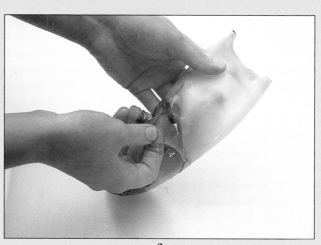

3

Peel off the skin by pulling from the cut end to the tail. The squid is now ready for use.

Microwave Cooking

The microwave oven is an excellent appliance to use for both defrosting and cooking fish. Timing is critical when microwaving fish and will differ according to the output of your particular model. A 700w microwave will cook faster than a 500w model. Remember also that the more you put into a microwave, the longer it will take to cook as the energy has to be shared between the amount of food in the cabinet. Standing time should also be considered, food continues to cook for a short period after being removed from the microwave and this must be allowed for when cooking fish. It is always better to undercook as you can pop the fish back into the oven for a minute or two after the standing time has ended, but if you overcook the fish initially, it will be spoiled.

Rules for Microwaving Fish

1. Arrange fish in a single layer in a shallow dish. Always cover during cooking, unless using a browning dish to achieve a crisp finish. Covering will help keep the fish moist, will speed up cooking time, keep the flavor in the fish and help prevent the oven from becoming dirty.

2. Always cook foods in non-metallic containers, this includes those which have a metal rim or trim.

3. Whether your particular model has a turntable or not, always turn the fish over once during cooking.

4. When cooking fish steaks, arrange them in a ring fashion, keeping thicker parts towards the outside edge of the dish.

5. If the recipe calls for it, remember to stir as in a fish stew or soup – stirring, and turning where stirring is not advisable, are important parts of microwave cooking and help to ensure even cooking results.

6. Always cook fish for the minimum advised cooking time – it can always go back in the microwave after the standing time if necessary.

7. Fish benefits by the addition of a little liquid – add water, stock or lemon juice.

8. Do not add salt before microwaving as it tends to cause dryness.

Defrosting Fish

Frozen fish may be successfully defrosted using the defrost control on your microwave. Always lay the fish out in a single layer in a covered dish and turn over once half way through defrosting. Follow the chart in the manufacturer's manual, supplied with your oven so that you have a guide as to timings. And allow a standing time between defrosting and cooking as the fish will continue to defrost during this time, just as it continues to cook after the cooking time.

Fish can be cooked straight from frozen on 100% Full power in the microwave, although generally, it is easier to achieve perfect results if the fish is defrosted first. To cook straight through from frozen, simply double the cooking time given for cooking fresh fish, checking frequently and

remembering to turn the fish during cooking and to allow a standing time at the end – 3 or 4 minutes standing is sufficient for most fish recipes.

Barbecuing

Barbecues or 'cook-outs' are popular social occasions – there are very few people who do not enjoy a glass of wine and the aroma of food cooking on the open fire. As barbecues are often held right on the shore, fish is one of the best foods to cook by this method.

Remember that fish barbecues quickly, so take care to oil the barbecue grill rack and kebab sticks or fish grids and either marinade white fish or brush with oil before cooking. Add a little seasoning and some fresh herbs before cooking to impart a delicate flavor to the flesh of the fish.

Choose firm fish that will not disintegrate during cooking and cut into thick fillets or thick chunks for kebabs or barbecue whole fish with the cleaned belly filled with herbs. Make 2 or 3 slashes in the skin of whole fish before cooking and turn 2 or 3 times. Small whole fish will benefit from being wrapped in foil parcels before grilling. They will take about 30 minutes, so cook them arranged towards the edge of the barbecue, and add herbs such as thyme and rosemary, seasoning and a little lemon juice to the parcels before closing them.

For a delicious marinade, combine ²/₃ cup dry cider with ¼ cup walnut or olive oil, 1 clove crushed garlic, and 1 tablespoon mixed, crushed fresh herbs such as rosemary, thyme and marjoram.

Add ¼ teaspoon salt and a little finely ground black pepper. Mix well and pour over the fish. This amount of marinade will be sufficient for 6 people.

Braising

As fish cooks quickly it may seem slightly unusual to think of a fish casserole. However, it is a good moist method of cooking some of the less expensive cuts of fish. By this method large chunks of fish are cooked on top of a selection of chopped root vegetables which have been stir-fried in a little melted butter until softened and starting to brown. Liquid in the form of stock, wine, cider or apple juice to just cover the fish is added, with a little seasoning and some fresh herbs.

The pan is then covered with a lid and left over a gentle heat until the fish is tender. Serve the fish with the accompanying vegetables and liquid – thicken the sauce after lifting the fish if desired, but if you serve chunks of fresh bread with the stew your family or guests can simply soak the wonderful juices up with the bread.

Baking

This is an ideal method of cooking whole fish and also excellent for large fillets or steaks of fish. Baked fish should be cooked in an oven preheated for 15 minutes to 375°F. Prepared whole fish is delicious cooked on its own, simply seasoned and stuffed with a few herbs – remember to slash the skin in two or three places to ensure even

grid over so that it is positioned at its lower level in the pan and then line it with foil before arranging the prepared fish onto the foil. This makes washing up much easier as the messy foil is simply screwed up and thrown away. The speed of cooking will vary according to your particular broiler and how near the fish is to the intense heat. The fish will need turning once or twice during cooking and remember to test frequently to see if the fish is cooked.

Fish is best cooked under a medium heat which allows the heat to penetrate more evenly right through to the center.

Deep-Fat Frying

Deep-fat frying is a fast method of cooking small whole fish such as whitebait. It is also a useful method of cooking small pieces of fish dipped in batter. The food is placed in a wire basket and lowered into a

cooking. Lay in a shallow dish and bake uncovered for 45-60 minutes, according to size, and baste one or twice with the resulting fish juice. Fillets or steaks of fish will benefit by the addition of a little liquid in the form of stock or wine and should be covered with a lid or some foil. Be careful not to overcook the fish – test frequently and remove as soon as the flesh flakes easily. Allow roughly 6-10 minutes per pound plus 6-10 minutes over, according to the thickness of the fillets.

Whole fish cooked by this method makes an attractive center piece for a buffet table and is often served cold, skinned and attractively garnished after cooking.

Broiling

This quick method of cooking is a popular way of dealing with fish

fillets, steaks, or small whole fish, such as anchovies.

The prepared fish should be seasoned and then brushed with a little oil. Try turning the broiler

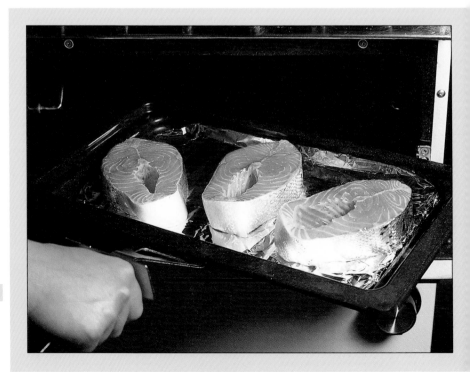

pan of oil which should come about ¾ of the way up the pan and be preheated to about 360°F. It is important that the oil is clean and of sufficient depth to cover the food. If the oil is not heated to sufficient temperature before the food is added, the resulting fish will be soggy, as the heat of the oil will not have immediately sealed the outside of the fish. However, if the oil is too hot, the outside of the food will burn before the inside has had time to cook.

Check the temperature of the oil with a cook's thermometer then you'll be sure of success!

As oil cooks food very quickly, fish, because of its very delicate nature, needs to have a protective coating added before it is exposed to the extreme temperature of the oil. The coating helps to stop the fish breaking up, and also acts as a flavor seal, locking the flavor into the food. Seasoned flour, batter or egg and breadcrumbs are all suitable coating for fish. Cook small quantities at a time so that the temperature of the oil is not reduced.

Once the fish is cooked (it will be golden and crisp) remove it immediately and drain on paper towels before serving with wedges of lemon.

Shallow Frying

Shallow frying is a quick method of cooking fairly small amounts of fillets, fish steaks and small whole fish such as herring and mackerel. The fish should be protected with some sort of coating – dipped in beaten egg and rolled in breadcrumbs is ideal or dipped in milk and then rolled in flour or

oatmeal. The oil should come just under half way up the pan and be heated until a shimmery haze rises from the pan. Add the fish and quickly seal on both sides then reduce heat slightly and cook until crisp and golden, turning once or twice. It is a good idea to cover the pan with a splatter guard to prevent splashing – this is a fine wire mesh cover with a heatproof handle designed to fit over the shallow frying pan completely during the frying process.

It prevents the fat splattering and is a definite advantage. Once the food is cooked it should be drained well on paper towels and served immediately.

Stir Frying

Stir frying is done in a large shallow frying pan, or ideally, in a wok. It is a useful method of cooking small pieces of fish or shellfish quickly.

Start by stir frying prepared vegetables such as onions and peppers in a little oil, then add the fish, which will cook in 30 seconds to 1 minute. An important factor in stir frying is that the ingredients are all assembled and prepared before the oil is heated. The vegetables should be cut into even-sized strips. The whole meal is cooked and served all from one pan in one pan and usually accompanied by boiled or fried rice. The food is simply cooked, by stirring continuously over a fairly high heat, using a slotted draining spoon. Soy sauce is often added before serving but there is a wide range of sauces such as oyster sauce, which are very tasty.

Poaching

Poaching is cooking gently in a liquid such as wine, water, fish stock or milk. Heat the liquid first then add the fish – both whole fish,

fillets and fish cutlets are excellent cooked by this method. Cook them in a single layer, allowing the liquid to come about ¾ of the way up the fish. Season and cover with a tightly-fitting lid and poach small fillets and cutlets for about 8 minutes, whole fish may take 15-20 minutes.

Check continually, as when cooking fish by any other method and remove with the flesh in the thickest part of the fish flakes easily. The liquid should be used to make an accompanying sauce or reserved and used for a fish soup.

Steaming

Steaming is an easy method of cooking fish fillets which ensures the fish remains juicy as it is surrounded by moisture whilst cooking. Here again care should always be taken not to overcook. The fillet should be rolled or folded, lightly seasoned and steamed for 10-15 minutes in a steamer, covered with a closely fitted lid, over simmering water. If no steamer is available, steam the fish between 2 dinner plates over a pan of simmering water. Steamed

fish is full of flavor. Serve it on its own with freshly cooked vegetables in season, accompanied by a light parsley or cheese sauce, if required. The fish can also be steamed over water containing herbs to give a subtle flavour.

There's very little that can go wrong when steaming fish, simply ensure that there is sufficient water in the pan and that it is maintained at simmering point throughout the cooking process. Also, make sure that you cover the fish with a tightly-fitting lid, so that the steam which actually cooks the fish is kept in.

Fish Stock

A good basic fish stock can be made for almost nothing, using fish head, skin and bones supplied by your fishmonger. It is far quicker to make than meat stock, taking only 10-15 minutes and makes a delicately flavored base for all types of sauces. To prepare the stock put the fish heads, bones and skins into a large saucepan, add a bouquet garnis with some seasoning. Cover bones etc. with cold water and simmer gently in the covered pan for 10-15 minutes. Strain and use as required.

Fish Soup

Fish soup deserves to be served more often. It is warming, nourishing and delicious. Fresh bread is all that is needed to turn fish soup into a filling and economical meal which is easy to prepare. Fish soups offer great scop for variety. Start with a simple recipe and then develop it using your own favorite ingredients.

Accompaniments for Fish

There is simply nothing to equal the flavor of freshly caught fish, well cooked and served with a garnish of fresh lemon or lime and accompanied by a selection of fresh vegetables. However, there are many occasions when the addition of a well chosen sauce will greatly enhance a fish dish, so simply choose one of the following to serve with your favorite fish – your guests will be doubly impressed.

Coating Sauces

A coating sauce is made from a roux base and is designed to lightly coat the fish or vegetables with which it is to be served. It should be carefully prepared in a thick pan and served as soon as it is ready – a correctly made coating sauce should be of the consistency of thick cream and coat the back of a wooden spoon. The sauce may be varied considerably according to the type of liquid used in making it e.g.. white wine, fish stock, milk or light cream, and the type of flavorings e.g.. fresh parsley, cheese, curry powder, finely

chopped button mushrooms, cooked chopped onion, cooked chopped shrimps etc.

White Sauce

Serves 4

3 tbsps butter
6 tbsps white, all-purpose flour
2 cups whole milk
Salt and freshly ground black
  pepper

Melt the butter in a heavy saucepan, stir in the flour to form a roux and cook over a gentle heat, stirring, for 2 minutes.

Remove pan from heat and blend in a little of the milk, using a balloon whisk. Add the rest of the milk, gradually, whisking continually to ensure there are no lumps. Season.

Return to heat and bring to the boil, stirring all the time. Simmer gently for 5 minutes, stirring. Serve immediately.

Variations: To the above coating sauce one of the following may be added:-

Curry Sauce: Add 1 tsp curry powder, mixed with the flour.

Parsley Sauce: Add 1 tbsp freshly chopped parsley to the prepared sauce, just before serving.

Cheese Sauce: Add ¾ cup freshly grated, mature Cheddar cheese to the freshly made sauce. Stir to melt, then serve immediately.

Mushroom Sauce: Add ½ cup finely chopped button mushrooms to the prepared sauce. The mushrooms will cook in the intense heat of the sauce. Serve immediately.

Shrimp Sauce: Add ½ cup cooked, shelled shrimp to the completed sauce. Heat through gently over a low heat, stirring continuously, until very hot. Serve immediately.

Egg Sauce: Hard-cook, peel and finely chop 2 eggs and add to the sauce.

Onion Sauce: Add 1 medium onion, finely chopped and softened in a medium pan in 2 tbsps melted butter, to the completed sauce. Serve immediately.

Hollandaise Sauce

Serves 4

Serve this piquant sauce warm, rather than hot, with all types of fish. It is a particularly rich sauce and ideal on a special buffet table accompanying a whole, dressed salmon or a colorful mixed seafood platter.

3 tbsps tarragon vinegar
1 tbsp water
2 egg yolks
6 tbsps butter
Salt and freshly ground black
  pepper

Put vinegar and water into a small non-stick pan and bring to the boil. Boil until reduced to about 1 tablespoon. Remove from heat and allow to cool slightly. Put the egg yolks into a bowl and stir in the vinegar. Set over a pan of hot water and heat gently, stirring all the time, until the egg mixture thickens. (Keep the water just gently simmering so that the egg does not overcook.) Divide butter into small pieces and gradually whisk into the sauce. Season to taste. The sauce should be the consistency of home-made

mayonnaise and golden yellow in color. It should be slightly piquant in flavor.

Tartar Sauce

Serves 4

This popular sauce is traditionally served with fried fish and chips.

1¼ cups home-made mayonnaise
  (see recipe)
2½ tsps chopped gherkins
2½ tsps chopped capers
½ cup natural yogurt or light
  cream
1 tsp freshly chopped parsley or
  basil

Mix all ingredients together. Cover and refrigerate until ready to serve.

Gooseberry Sauce

Serves 4

This unusual sauce is pleasantly tart and therefore particularly good served with oily fish such as trout, mackerel and salmon. It may be made in advance and reheated just before serving. This sauce also freezes well.

15oz can gooseberries in natural
  juice
Grated rind ½ lemon
2½ tsps lemon juice
2½ tsps superfine sugar
2 tbsps butter

Liquidize or process the gooseberries with their juice, until puréed. Turn into a medium saucepan. Add the lemon rind, juice, the sugar and the butter. Heat, over a medium heat, stirring constantly until simmering. Serve with fish of your choice.

Yogurt Sauce with Celery

Serves 4

A light, creamy sauce which is ideal to serve with fish kebabs, grilled salmon or whole, baked fish.

²/₃ cup natural yogurt
1 tsp concentrated mint sauce
1 tsp lemon juice
1 tsp clear honey
6 tbsps light cream
2 sticks celery, finely chopped

Mix all ingredients, except the celery, until well blended. Add celery and serve immediately.

Mayonnaise

Serves 4

Mayonnaise is simple to make using an electric blender or food processor. It can be varied in many ways according to taste and makes an excellent accompaniment to just about any fish dish.

1 tsp freshly-made English mustard
1 egg
1 egg yolk
3 tbsps lemon juice
1¼ cups sunflower or grapeseed oil
Salt and freshly ground black pepper

Put the mustard, egg and egg yolk into the blender or food processor bowl. Blend or process for about 15 seconds. Leave the machine running and very slowly add the oil, a drop at a time at first, then slightly faster. Continue to process until the mayonnaise is thick and creamy. Add lemon juice and seasoning and process for a few seconds longer. Serve immediately or keep for up to 2 weeks in a screw-top jar in the refrigerator.

Variations

Curry Mayonnaise: Add 1 teaspoon curry powder or paste instead of the mustard.

Parsley Mayonnaise: Stir 1 tablespoon freshly chopped parsley into the prepared mayonnaise.

Tomato Mayonnaise: Add 1-2 tablespoons tomato purée to the mayonnaise when you add the lemon juice.

Garlic Mayonnaise: Add 3 cloves crushed garlic when you add the lemon juice.

Lemon and Basil Mayonnaise: Add grated rind of ½ lemon and 2 teaspoons finely chopped fresh basil when you add the lemon juice.

Bouillabaisse

Serves 4

4 tbsps butter
1 stick celery, chopped
1 medium onion, chopped
1 clove garlic, crushed
1lb tomatoes, peeled and chopped
1lb white fish, such as cod
1 bouquet garni
Salt and freshly ground black pepper
½ cup dry cider
5 cups boiling water
1 x 7oz can tuna fish in brine, drained
4oz cooked shrimp
Freshly chopped parsley to garnish

Melt the butter in a large pan, then soften the celery, onion and garlic over a medium heat. Add the tomatoes and continue to cook, stirring occasionally for a further 5 minutes. Add the prepared white fish, cut into neat chunks with the bouquet garni, seasoning, and the cider. Pour on the boiling water. Cover with a lid, bring to the boil and boil fairly briskly for about 15 minutes. Add the flaked tuna and the shrimp and heat gently for 3 minutes. Remove bouquet garni, then using a draining spoon, lift fish and divide between soup dishes. Add liquid, then garnish with parsley and serve immediately.

Fish Chowder

Serves 4

1lb white fish fillets, washed
1¼ cups milk
Salt and freshly ground black pepper
2 strips bacon, de-rinded and chopped
1 tbsp butter
8oz potato, peeled and diced
2 medium carrots, diced
1 medium onion, chopped
1¾ cups chicken stock, boiling
3 tbsps cornstarch
Chopped parsley to garnish

Put fish into a saucepan with half the milk and simmer gently for 10 minutes. Drain fish, retaining milk and set aside, covered. Fry bacon in a clean, non-stick medium saucepan until crisp, add butter, then when melted, add onion and fry to soften. Add potato and carrot with reserved milk, remaining milk and the stock, simmer gently for 10-15 minutes, until potato and carrot are tender. Blend cornstarch with a little water and stir into the pan. Simmer for 5 minutes, stirring. Add fish with any juices, re-heat gently until thoroughly hot, and serve immediately, sprinkled with plenty of freshly chopped parsley.

Chapter I

Soups
&
Appetizers

SERVES 6-8

CLAM CHOWDER

French fishermen invented this thick soup-stew, but New Englanders adopted it as their own, using the delicious varieties of clams found along their coastlines.

2lbs clams (1lb shelled or canned clams)
3oz rindless bacon, diced
2 medium onions, finely diced
1 tbsp flour
6 medium potatoes, peeled and cubed
Salt and pepper
4 cups milk
1 cup milk
1 cup light cream
Chopped parsley (optional)

Step 2 Cook the bacon slowly until the fat renders.

Step 3 Cook the onion in the bacon fat until soft and translucent.

Step 1 Cook the clams until the shells open. Stir occasionally for even cooking.

1. Scrub the clams well and place them in a basin of cold water with a handful of flour to soak for 30 minutes. Drain the clams and place them in a deep saucepan with about ½ cup cold water. Cover and bring to the boil, stirring occasionally until all the shells open. Discard any shells that do not open. Strain the clam liquid and reserve it and set the clams aside to cool.

2. Place the diced bacon in a large, deep saucepan and cook slowly until the fat is rendered. Turn up the heat and brown the bacon. Remove it to paper towel to drain.

3. Add the onion to the bacon fat in the pan and cook slowly to soften. Stir in the flour and add the potatoes, salt, pepper, milk and reserved clam juice.

4. Cover and bring to the boil and cook for about 10 minutes, or until the potatoes are nearly tender. Remove the clams from their shells and chop them if large. Add to the soup along with the cream and diced bacon. Cook a further 10 minutes, or until the potatoes and clams are tender. Add the chopped parsley, if desired, and serve immediately.

Cook's Notes

Time
Preparation takes about 30 minutes and cooking takes about 20 minutes.

Cook's Tip
Soaking clams and other shellfish in water with flour or cornmeal before cooking plumps them up and also helps to eliminate sand and grit.

Buying Guide
If fresh or canned clams are not available, substitute mussels or cockles instead.

SERVES 4

HOT AND SOUR SEAFOOD SOUP

This interesting combination of flavors and ingredients makes a sophisticated beginning to an informal meal.

3 dried Chinese mushrooms
1 tbsp vegetable oil
¾ cup shrimp, shelled and deveined
1 red chili, seeded and finely sliced
1 green chili, seeded and finely sliced
½ tsp lemon rind, cut into thin slivers
2 green onions, sliced
2 cups fish stock
1 tbsp Worcestershire sauce
1 tbsp light soy sauce
2oz whitefish fillets
1 cake of fresh bean curd, diced
1 tbsp lemon juice
1 tsp sesame seeds
Salt and pepper
1 tsp fresh coriander, finely chopped (optional)

Step 1 Soak the dried Chinese mushrooms in boiling water for about 20 minutes, until they are completely reconstituted.

1. Soak the mushrooms in enough hot water to cover for 20 minutes, or until completely reconstituted.

2. Heat the vegetable oil in a large wok or frying pan, and add the shrimp, chilies, lemon rind and green onions. Stir-fry quickly for 1 minute.

3. Add the stock, the Worcestershire sauce and the soy sauce. Bring this mixture to the boil, reduce the heat and simmer for 5 minutes. Season to taste.

4. Remove the hard stalks from the mushrooms and discard them. Slice the caps very finely.

5. Cut the whitefish fillets into small dice, and add them to the soup, together with the bean curd and Chinese mushrooms. Simmer for a further 5 minutes.

6. Stir in the lemon juice and sesame seeds. Adjust the seasoning and serve sprinkled with chopped fresh coriander leaves, if desired.

Step 4 Remove the hard stalks from the reconstituted Chinese mushrooms and discard them. Slice the caps finely.

Step 5 Cut the fish fillets into small dice, and add these to the soup mixture, together with the bean curd and shredded mushroom caps.

Cook's Notes

Time
Preparation takes about 20 minutes, and cooking also takes about 20 minutes.

Cook's Tip
Dried Chinese mushrooms and fresh bean curd cakes can be bought in most delicatessens, or ethnic supermarkets.

Watchpoint
Care must be taken when using fresh chilies not to get the juice into the eyes or the mouth. If this should happen, rinse with lots of cold water.

SERVES 6

SHRIMP BISQUE

This classic Cajun recipe makes a first
course or a full meal. It isn't a smooth
purée like its French counterpart.

3 tbsps butter or margarine
1 onion, finely chopped
1 red pepper, seeded and finely chopped
2 sticks celery, finely chopped
1 clove garlic, minced
Pinch dry mustard and cayenne pepper
2 tsps paprika
3 tbsps flour
4 cups fish stock
1 sprig thyme and bay leaf
8oz raw, peeled shrimp
Salt and pepper
Snipped chives

3. Pour on the stock gradually, stirring until well blended.
Add the thyme and bay leaf and bring to the boil. Reduce
the heat and simmer about 5 minutes or until thickened,
stirring occasionally.

4. Add the shrimp and cook until pink and curled, about 5
minutes. Season with salt and pepper to taste and top with
snipped chives before serving.

Step 3 Pour on
the stock
gradually and stir
or whisk until well
blended.

Step 2 Cook the
mustard, cayenne,
paprika and flour
briefly until the
mixture darkens in
color.

Step 4 Use
kitchen scissors to
snip the chives
finely over the top
of the soup before
serving.

1. Melt the butter or margarine and add the onion, pepper,
celery and garlic. Cook gently to soften.

2. Stir in the mustard, cayenne, paprika and flour. Cook
about 3 minutes over gentle heat, stirring occasionally.

Cook's Notes

Time
Preparation takes about 20
minutes and cooking takes
about 8-10 minutes.

Variation
If using peeled, cooked
shrimp add just before serving
and heat through for about 2 minutes
only.

Cook's Tip
Cook spices such as paprika
briefly before adding any
liquid to develop their flavor and
eliminate harsh taste.

SERVES 4

CREOLE COURT BOUILLON

Different from a gumbo, this is still a classic Creole
soup-stew. Usually, it's prepared with redfish, local
to the region, but any firm whitefish will substitute.

Fishbones
1 bay leaf, 1 sprig thyme and 2 parsley stalks
2 slices onion
1 lemon slice
6 black peppercorns
1½ cups water
6 tbsps oil
6 tbsps flour
1 large green pepper, seeded and finely chopped
1 onion, finely chopped
1 stick celery, finely chopped
2lbs canned tomatoes
2 tbsps tomato paste
1 tsp cayenne pepper
Pinch salt and allspice
6 tbsps white wine
2 whole plaice, filleted and skinned
2 tbsps chopped parsley

Step 4 Pour the
fish stock onto the
brown roux,
whisking
constantly to form
a smooth paste.

1. Prepare the fish stock as in the recipe for Poisson en
Papillote.

2. Heat the oil and add the flour. Cook slowly, stirring
constantly, until golden brown

3. Add the green pepper, onion and celery, and cook until
the flour is a rich dark brown and the vegetables have
softened.

4. Strain on the stock and add the canned tomatoes,
tomato paste, cayenne pepper, salt and allspice. Bring to
the boil and then simmer until thick. Add the wine.

5. Cut the fish fillets into 2 inch pieces and add to the
tomato mixture. Cook slowly for about 20 minutes, or until
the fish is tender. Gently stir in the parsley, taking care that
the fish does not break up. Adjust the seasoning and serve.

Step 4 Simmer
the tomato
mixture until very
thick.

Step 5 Cut the
fish fillets into 2
inch pieces and
add to the tomato
mixture.

Cook's Notes

Time
Preparation takes about 30
minutes and cooking takes
about 20 minutes for the fish stock and
20 minutes to finish the dish.

Preparation
Fish stock can be prepared a
day in advance and
refrigerated. It can also be frozen.

Variation
Shrimp may be added if
desired.

SERVES 4-6

CRAB & SWEETCORN SOUP

Creamy sweetcorn and succulent crabmeat
combine to make a velvety rich soup. Whisked
egg whites add an interesting texture.

3½ cups chicken or fish stock
12oz cream style corn
4oz crabmeat
Salt and pepper
1 tsp light soy sauce
2 tbsps cornstarch
3 tbsps water or stock
4 green onions for garnish
2 egg whites, whisked
4 green onions for garnish

Step 3 Whisk the egg whites until soft peaks form and stir into the hot soup.

Step 2 Mix the cornstarch and water together with some of the hot soup and return the mixture to the pan.

1. Bring the stock to the boil in a large pan. Add the corn, crabmeat, seasoning and soy sauce. Allow to simmer for 4-5 minutes.

2. Mix the cornstarch and water or stock and add a spoonful of the hot soup. Return the mixture to the soup and bring back to the boil. Cook until the soup thickens.

3. Whisk the egg whites until soft peaks form. Stir into the hot soup just before serving.

4. Slice the onions thinly on the diagonal and scatter over the top to serve.

Cook's Notes

 Time
Preparation takes about 10 minutes, cooking takes about 8-10 minutes.

 Preparation
Adding the egg whites is optional.

 Watchpoint
Do not allow the corn and the crab to boil rapidly; they will both toughen.

 Economy
Use crab sticks instead of crabmeat.

 Variation
Chicken may be used instead of the crabmeat and the cooking time increased to 10-12 minutes.

SERVES 4

NEW ENGLAND BOUILLABAISSE

French settlers brought this favorite recipe to the New World, and just as they would have at home, they used local, seasonal ingredients in it.

Stock

1lb fish bones, skin and heads
7 cups water
1 small onion, thinly sliced
1 small carrot, thinly sliced
1 bay leaf
6 black peppercorns
1 blade mace
1 sprig thyme
1 lemon slices

Bouillabaisse

⅓ cup butter or margarine
1 carrot, sliced
3 leeks, well washed and thinly sliced
1 clove garlic
Pinch saffron
⅓-½ cup dry white wine
8oz canned tomatoes
1 lobster
1lb cod or halibut fillets
1lb mussels, well scrubbed
1lb small clams, well scubbed
8 new potatoes, scrubbed but not peeled
Chopped parsley
8oz large shrimp, peeled and de-veined

1. First prepare the fish stock. Place all the stock ingredients in a large stock pot and bring to the boil over high heat. Lower the heat and allow to simmer for 20 minutes. Strain and reserve the stock. Discard the fish bones and vegetables.

2. Melt the butter in a medium-sized saucepan and add the carrots, leeks and garlic. Cook for about 5 minutes until slightly softened.

3. Add the saffron and wine and allow to simmer for about 5 minutes.

4. Add the fish stock along with all the remaining bouillabaisse ingredients except the shrimp. Bring the mixture to the boil and cook until the lobster turns red, the mussel and clam shells open and the potatoes are tender. Turn off the heat and add the shrimp. Cover the pan and let the shrimp cook in the residual heat. Divide the ingredients among 4 soup bowls. Remove the lobster and cut it in half. Divide the tail between the other 2 bowls and serve the bouillabaisse with garlic bread.

Step 2 Cook the carrots, leeks and garlic in butter until soft but not colored. Combine all the bouillabaisse ingredients in a large stock pot.

Step 4 Remove the lobster and cut it in half using a large, sharp knife.

Cook's Notes

Time
Preparation takes about 35 minutes and cooking takes about 30 minutes.

Watchpoint
Leeks must be split in half first and rinsed under cold water to remove sand and grit before slicing.

Variation
Use whatever shellfish or fish is in season or suits your taste. Lobster is not essential.

SERVES 2-4

SEA ISLAND SHRIMP

Although this is a recipe from the
Carolinas, it is popular everywhere
succulent shrimp are available.

2 dozen raw large shrimp, unpeeled
4 tbsps butter or margarine
1 small red pepper, seeded and finely chopped
2 green onions, finely chopped
½ tsp dry mustard
2 tsps dry sherry
1 tsp Worcester sauce
4oz cooked crab meat
6 tbsps fresh breadcrumbs
1 tbsp chopped parsley
2 tbsps mayonnaise
Salt and pepper
1 small egg, beaten
Grated Parmesan cheese
Paprika

1. Remove all of the shrimp shells except for the very tail ends.

2. Remove the black veins on the rounded sides.

3. Cut the shrimp down the length of the curved side and press each one open.

4. Melt half of the butter or margarine in a small pan and cook the pepper to soften, about 3 minutes. Add the green onions and cook a further 2 minutes.

5. Combine the peppers with the mustard, sherry, Worcester sauce, crab meat, breadcrumbs, parsley and mayonnaise. Add seasoning and enough egg to bind together.

6. Spoon the stuffing onto the shrimp and sprinkle with the Parmesan cheese and paprika. Melt the remaining butter or margarine and drizzle over the shrimp.

7. Bake in a pre-heated 350°F oven for about 10 minutes. Serve immediately.

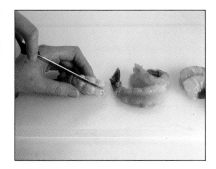

Step 3 Cut the shrimp down the length of the curved side and press each one open.

Step 6 Spoon the stuffing into the shrimp, pressing down lightly to spread shrimp open.

 *Cook's Notes*

 Time
Preparation takes about 30 minutes and cooking takes about 15 minutes.

 Variation
Try chopped black or green olives in the stuffing for a change of flavor. Mushrooms may be cooked with the red pepper and green onions, if desired, and other herbs substituted for parsley.

 Serving Ideas
Serve as an appetizer or as a main course for 2 people.

SERVES 6-8

CRAB MEAT BALLS

Delicious as a first course or a cocktail
snack, crab meat balls can be made ahead,
then coated and fried at the last minute.

1lb fresh or frozen crab meat, chopped finely
4 slices white bread, crusts removed and made into
  crumbs
1 tbsp butter or margarine
1 tbsp flour
½ cup milk
½ red or green chili, seeded and finely chopped
1 green onion, finely chopped
1 tbsp chopped parsley
Salt
Flour
2 eggs, beaten
Dry breadcrumbs
Oil for frying

Step 4 Flour hands well and shape cold crab mixture into balls.

Step 5 Brush on beaten egg or dip into egg to coat.

1. Combine the crab meat with the fresh breadcrumbs and set aside.

2. Melt the butter and add the flour off the heat. Stir in the milk and return to moderate heat. Bring to the boil, stirring constantly.

3. Stir the white sauce into the crab meat and breadcrumbs, adding the chili, onion and parsley. Season with salt to taste, cover and allow to cool completely.

4. Shape the cold mixture into 1 inch balls with floured hands.

5. Coat with beaten egg using a fork to turn balls in the mixture or use a pastry brush to coat with egg.

6. Coat with the dry breadcrumbs.

7. Fry in oil in a deep sauté pan, saucepan or deep-fat fryer at 350°F until golden brown and crisp, about 3 minutes per batch of 6. Turn occasionally while frying.

8. Drain on paper towels and sprinkle lightly with salt.

Cook's Notes

 Time
Preparation takes about 40-50 minutes, including time for the mixture to cool. A batch of 6 balls takes about 3 minutes to cook.

 Variation
Use finely chopped shrimp instead of crab meat. Omit chili if desired, or use a quarter red or green pepper.

$ **Economy**
Cooked whitefish such as haddock or whiting can be substituted for half of the crab meat. Crab sticks can also be used.

SERVES 4

OYSTERS ROCKEFELLER

Oysters can be purchased already opened, and
you'll find the rest of this famous New
Orleans dish simplicity itself to prepare.

24 oysters on the half shell
Rock salt
6 strips bacon, finely chopped
1¼ lbs fresh spinach, well washed, stems removed and
    leaves finely chopped
1 small bunch green onions, finely chopped
2 cloves garlic, crushed
4-5 tbsps fine fresh breadcrumbs
Dash tabasco
2 tbsps aniseed liqueur
Pinch salt
Parmesan cheese

1. Loosen the oysters from their shells, strain and reserve
their liquid.

2. Rinse the shells well and return an oyster to each one.
Pour about 1 inch of rock salt into a baking pan and place
in the oysters in their shells, pressing each shell gently into
the salt.

3. Place the bacon in a large frying pan and cook slowly to
render the fat. Turn up the heat and brown the bacon
evenly.

4. Add the spinach, green onions and garlic and cook
slowly until softened. Add the breadcrumbs, tabasco,
oyster liquid, liqueur, and a pinch of salt.

5. Spoon some of the mixture onto each oyster and
sprinkle with Parmesan cheese. Place in a preheated
350°F oven for about 15 minutes. Alternatively, heat
through in the oven for 10 minutes and place under a
preheated broiler to lightly brown the cheese. Serve
immediately.

Step 1 With a small sharp knife, loosen the oysters from their shells to make them easier to eat. Hold over bowl to catch liquid.

Step 2 Press the oyster shells into a baking pan filled with salt so that the shells sit level.

Step 5 Spoon in the prepared mixture to cover each oyster completely.

Cook's Notes

Time
Preparation takes about 25
minutes or longer if opening
the oysters yourself. Cooking takes
about 25 minutes.

Buying Guide
It is possible to purchase
oysters already on the half
shell. If you need to open them yourself, buy a special oyster knife with a
short, strong blade.

Variation
Finely chopped anchovies
may be used instead of the
bacon, and 3 tbsps butter or margarine
substituted for the bacon fat.

SERVES 2-4

CRAB MEAT IMPERIAL

Another of New Orleans' famous dishes, this
makes a delicious warm weather salad for
lunches, light suppers or elegant appetizers.

2 small crabs, boiled
2 tbsps oil
4 green onions
1 small green pepper, seeded and finely chopped
1 stick celery, finely chopped
1 clove garlic, crushed
¾ cup prepared mayonnaise
1 tbsp mild mustard
Dash tabasco and Worcestershire sauce
1 piece canned pimento, drained and finely chopped
2 tbsps chopped parsley
Salt and pepper
Lettuce, curly endive or raddichio (optional)

1. To shell the crabs, first remove all the legs and the large claws by twisting and pulling them away from the body.

2. Turn the shell over and, using your thumbs, push the body away from the flat shell. Set the body aside.

3. Remove the stomach sack and the lungs or dead man's fingers and discard them. Using a small teaspoon, scrape the brown body meat out of the flat shell.

4. Using a sharp knife, cut the body of the crab in four pieces and using a pick or a skewer, push out all the meat.

5. Crack the large claws and remove the meat in one piece if possible. Crack the legs and remove the meat as well, leaving the small, thin legs in the shell. Set all the meat aside. Scrub the shells if desired to use for serving.

6. Heat the oil in a small sauté pan or frying pan. Chop the white parts of the green onions and add to the oil with the green pepper, celery and garlic. Sauté over gentle heat for about 10 minutes, stirring often to soften the vegetables but not brown them. Remove from the heat and set aside. When cool, add the mayonnaise, mustard, tabasco,

Worcestershire sauce, pimento and finely chopped tops of the green onions.

7. Spoon the reserved brown body meat from the crabs back into each shell or serving dish. Mix the remaining crab meat with the dressing, reserving the crab claws for garnish, if desired. They may also be shredded and added to the other crab meat. Do not overmix the sauce as the crab meat should stay in large pieces. Spoon into the shells on top of the brown body meat, sprinkle with chopped parsley and place the crab shells on serving plates, surrounding them with lettuce leaves, if desired. Garnish with the shelled crab claws and use the crab legs if desired. Sprinkle with parsley and serve immediately.

Step 3 Discard the plastic-like stomach sack and spongy lungs. Remove brown body meat from the shell of the crab and reserve it.

Step 4 Cut through the body of the crab with a sharp knife and pick out the crab meat with a skewer.

Cook's Notes

Time
Preparation takes about 45 minutes, cooking takes about 10 minutes.

Variation
If desired, recipe can be prepared with dressed or frozen crab meat. Allow about 3-4 oz crab meat per person.

Buying Guide
Precooked crabs may be purchased from fishmongers or fish markets. Use on the day of purchase.

SERVES 4

MUSSELS IN RED WINE

Red wine makes an unusual, but very pleasant, combination with seafood. This recipe is equally good with clams.

3lb mussels, well scrubbed
1 cup dry red wine
6 tbsps olive oil
4 cloves garlic, finely chopped
2 bay leaves
2 tbsps fresh thyme, chopped
6 tbsps red wine vinegar
1 tsp paprika
Grated rind and juice of 1 lemon
Salt and pepper
Pinch cayenne pepper
Pinch sugar (optional)
Chopped parsley

1. Prepare the mussels as in the recipe for Paella. Place the wine in a large saucepan and bring to the boil. Add the mussels, cover the pan and cook briskly for about 4-5 minutes, stirring frequently, until the shells open. Discard any that do not open.

2. Transfer the mussels to a bowl and pour the cooking liquid through a fine strainer and reserve it.

3. In a clean saucepan, heat the oil and fry the garlic over gentle heat until golden brown. Add the bay leaves, thyme, vinegar, paprika, lemon juice and rind, salt, pepper and cayenne pepper. Pour on the wine, add sugar, if using, and bring to the boil. Cook to reduce to about ⅔ cup. Allow to cool completely.

4. Remove the mussels from their shells and add them to the liquid, stirring to coat all the mussels. Cover and place in the refrigerator for at least 2 hours. Allow to stand at room temperature for about 30 minutes before serving. Sprinkle with parsley.

Step 1
Cook the mussels over high heat, stirring frequently, until the shells begin to open.

Step 2
Transfer the mussels to a plate and pour the liquid through a fine strainer or through muslin.

Step 4
Remove the mussels from their shells with your fingers or by using a small teaspoon.

Cook's Notes

Time
Preparation takes about 30 minutes and cooking takes about 9-10 minutes.

Serving Ideas
Serve in small dishes as tapas. To serve as a more formal first course, place lettuce leaves on individual plates and spoon on the mussels. Sprinkle with chopped parsley, if desired.

Variation
If using frozen mussels, allow a further 2-3 minutes cooking time.

SERVES 4

FRIED FISH WITH GARLIC SAUCE

Fish in such an attractive shape makes an
excellent first course.

2lbs fresh anchovies or whitebait
1 cup of all-purpose flour
4-6 tbsps cold water
Pinch salt
Oil for frying

Garlic Sauce

4 slices bread, crusts trimmed, soaked in water for 10
    minutes
4 cloves garlic, peeled and roughly chopped
2 tbsps lemon juice
4-5 tbsps olive oil
1-2 tbsps water (optional)
Salt and pepper
2 tsps chopped fresh parsley
Lemon wedges for garnishing (optional)

1. Sift the flour into a deep bowl with a pinch of salt.
Gradually stir in the water in the amount needed to make a
very thick batter.

2. Heat enough oil for frying in a large, deep pan. A deep-
sided sauté pan is ideal.

3. Take 3 fish at a time and dip them into the batter together.
Press their tails together firmly to make a fan shape.

4. Lower them carefully into the oil. Fry in several batches
until crisp and golden. Continue in the same way with all the
remaining fish.

Step 3 Dip three
fish at a time into
the batter and
when coated
press the tails
together firmly to
form a fan shape.

Step 4 Lower the
fish carefully into
the hot oil to
preserve the
shape.

5. Meanwhile, squeeze out the bread and place in a food
processor with the garlic and lemon juice. With the processor running, add the oil in a thin, steady stream. Add
water if the mixture is too thick and dry. Add salt and pepper
and stir in the parsley by hand. When all the fish are cooked,
sprinkle lightly with salt and arrange on serving plates with
some of the garlic sauce and lemon wedges, if desired.

Cook's Notes

Time
Preparation takes about 30
minutes, cooking takes about
3 minutes per batch for the fish.

Preparation
Coat the fish in the batter just
before ready for frying.

Cook's Tip
The fish should be eaten
immediately after frying. If it is
necessary to keep the fish warm, place
them on a wire cooling rack covered
with paper towels in a slow oven with
the door open. Sprinkling fried food
lightly with salt helps to absorb excess
fat.

Variation
Fish may be dipped in the
batter and fried singly if
desired. Other fish, such as smelt or
sardines, may also be used. Use thin
strips of cod or halibut as well. Vary the
amount of garlic in the sauce to your
own taste.

SERVES 4

FRIED SQUID

Serve this sweet and delicious seafood
as an appetizer or main course. It's
easier to prepare than you think!

1½lb fresh squid
½ cup all-purpose flour
Salt and pepper
Oil for deep-frying
Lemon wedges and parsley for garnishing

1. Hold the body of the squid with one hand and the head with the other and pull gently to separate. Remove the intestines and the quill, which is clear and plastic-like. Rinse the body of the squid inside and outside under cold running water.

2. Cut the tentacles from the head, just above the eye. Separate into individual tentacles.

3. Remove the brownish or purplish outer skin from the body of the squid and cut the flesh into ¼ inch rings.

4. Mix the flour, salt and pepper together on a sheet of paper or in a shallow dish. Toss the rings of squid and the tentacles in the flour mixture to coat. Heat the oil to 350°F and fry the squid, about 6 pieces at a time, saving the tentacles until last. Remove them from the oil when brown and crisp with a draining spoon and place on paper towels.

Step 2 Cut the tentacles from the head just below the eye and separate them into individual pieces.

Step 3 Remove the outer skin from the body of the squid and cut the body into thin rings.

Sprinkle lightly with salt and continue with the remaining squid. The pieces will take about 3 minutes to cook. Place on serving dishes and garnish each dish with a wedge of lemon and some parsley.

Cook's Notes

Time
Preparation takes about 25 minutes, cooking takes 3 minutes per batch of 6 pieces.

Serving Ideas
Sprinkle the squid with chopped fresh oregano just before serving.

Preparation
Do not coat the pieces of squid too soon before frying or they will become soggy.

Watchpoint
Once the squid is added to the hot oil, cover the fryer as the oil will tend to spatter.

Cook's Tip
If the squid must be re-heated, spread the pieces on wire cooling racks covered with paper towels and place in a slow oven for about 10 minutes. Do not re-fry, as this toughens the squid.

SERVES 4-6

SWORDFISH KEBABS

Swordfish is one of the most commonly caught fish
in Southern Italy and Sicily. It won't fall apart
during cooking − a bonus when making kebabs.

2¼lbs swordfish steaks
6 tbsps olive oil
1 tsp chopped oregano
1 tsp chopped marjoram
Juice and rind of ½ a lemon
4 tomatoes, cut in thick slices
2 lemons, cut in thin slices
Salt and freshly ground pepper
Lemon slices and Italian parsley for garnish

1. Cut the swordfish steaks into 2 inch pieces.

2. Mix the olive oil, herbs, lemon juice and rind together
and set it aside. Thread the swordfish, tomato slices and
lemon slices on skewers, alternating the ingredients. Brush
the skewers with the oil and lemon juice mixture and cook
under a preheated broiler for about 10 minutes, basting
frequently with the lemon and oil. Serve garnished with
lemons and parsley.

Step 1 Cut the
swordfish steaks
into even-sized
pieces.

Step 2 Thread
the ingredients
onto the skewers,
alternating the
colors.

Cook's Notes

 Time
Preparation takes about 15
minutes, cooking takes about
10 minutes.

 Variations
Fresh tuna may be used
instead of swordfish. Use
cherry tomatoes instead of sliced
tomatoes, if available.

 Serving Ideas
Accompany the kebabs with
risotto and a green salad.

SERVES 4

MOULES MARINIÈRE

Brittany and Normandy are famous for mussels and for cream
and so cooks combined the two in one perfect seafood dish.

3lbs mussels
1½ cups dry cider or white wine
4 shallots, finely chopped
1 clove garlic, crushed
1 bouquet garni
½ cup heavy cream
3 tbsps butter, cut into small pieces
2 tbsps finely chopped parsley

1. Scrub the mussels well and remove the beards and any barnacles from the shells. Discard any mussels that have cracked shells and do not open when lightly tapped. Put the mussels into a large bowl and soak in cold water for at least 1 hour. Meanwhile, chop the parsley very finely.

2. Bring the cider or wine to the boil in a large stock pot and add the shallots, garlic and bouquet garni. Add the mussels, cover the pan and cook for 5 minutes. Shake the pan or stir the mussels around frequently until the shells open. Lift out the mussels into a large soup tureen or individual serving bowls. Discard any mussels that have not opened.

3. Reduce the cooking liquid by about half and strain into another saucepan. Add the cream and bring to the boil to thicken slightly. Beat in the butter, a few pieces at a time. Adjust the seasoning, add the parsley and pour the sauce over the mussels to serve.

Step 1 Break off thick stems from parsley and chop leaves very finely.

Step 2 Whilst cooking the mussels, stir or shake them frequently until the shells open.

Step 3 Beat the butter into the thickened cream and cooking liquid, a few pieces at a time.

Cook's Notes

Preparation
Soak mussels with a handful of flour or cornmeal in the water. They will then expel sand and take up the flour or cornmeal, which plumps them up.

Serving Ideas
Serve as a first course with French bread, or double the quantity of mussels to serve for a light main course.

Time
Preparation takes about 30 minutes, cooking takes about 15 minutes.

SERVES 4

FISH TEMPURA

This is a traditional Japanese dish, which can be served as
an unusual appetizer.

12 uncooked large shrimp
2 whitefish fillets, skinned and cut into 2 x ¾-inch strips
Small whole fish, e.g. smelt or whitebait
2 squid, cleaned and cut into strips 1x3 inches long
2 tbsps all-purpose flour, for dusting
1 egg yolk
Scant ½ cup iced water
1 cup all-purpose flour
Oil for frying
6 tbsps soy sauce
Juice and finely grated rind of 2 limes
4 tbsps dry sherry

1. Shell the shrimp, leaving the tails intact. Wash the fish
and the squid and pat dry. Dust them all with the 2 tbsps
flour.

2. Make a batter by beating together the egg yolk and
water. Sieve in the 1 cup of all-purpose flour and mix in well
with a table knife.

Step 2 The batter
will be lumpy and
look under mixed.

3. Dip each piece of fish into the batter, shaking off any
excess.

4. In a wok or deep-fat fryer, heat the oil to 350°F. Lower in
the fish pieces a few at a time and cook for 2-3 minutes. Lift
them out carefully and drain on paper towels, keeping
warm until required.

5. Mix together the soy sauce, lime juice, rind and sherry
and serve as a dip with the cooked fish.

Step 3 Do not
batter too many
pieces of fish at a
time. Only coat
those you are able
to cook.

Step 4 Cook only
3 or 4 pieces and
only one kind of
fish at a time.

Cook's Notes

Time
Preparation takes about 30
minutes and cooking time
varies from 2 to 3 minutes depending
on the type of fish.

Cook's Tip
If the batter seems to drain off
too quickly, leave each batch
of fish in the bowl of batter, until you are
ready to lower them into the hot oil.

Variation
Use a few vegetables, as well
as fish, for an interesting
change. Whole button mushrooms are
especially good.

SERVES 4

SALMON PÂTÉ

This highly nutritious, elegant pâté is low in fat and very
quick to prepare.

8oz canned red or pink salmon, drained
½ cup low fat curd cheese
Few drops lemon juice
Pinch ground mace, or ground nutmeg
¼ tsp Tabasco sauce
Freshly ground sea salt and black pepper
2 tbsps 1% fat fromage frais, or low fat yogurt
4 small pickles

1. Remove any bones and skin from the salmon. In a bowl,
work the fish into a smooth paste with the back of a spoon.

2. Beat the curd cheese until it is smooth.

3. Add the salmon, lemon juice, seasonings, and fromage
frais or natural yogurt to the curd cheese and mix well, until
thoroughly incorporated.

4. Divide the mixture equally between 4 individual custard
cups. Smooth the surfaces carefully.

5. Slice each pickle lengthways, 4 or 5 times, making sure
that you do not cut completely through the gherkin at the
narrow end. Splay the cut ends into a fan, and use these to

decorate the tops of the pâtés in the custard cups.

Step 1 Put the salmon into a small bowl and work it with the back of a spoon, until it becomes a smooth paste.

Step 5 Slice each pickle lengthways, 4 or 5 times, taking great care not to cut right through the pickle at the narrow end. Spread each of the cut ends out carefully into a fan shape. Use these to garnish the tops of the pâtés.

Cook's Notes

Time
Preparation takes about 15 minutes.

Preparation
If you have a food processor or liquidizer, you can work the curd cheese and salmon together in this, instead of beating them in a bowl.

Variation
Use canned tuna fish in place of the salmon.

Serving Ideas
Serve with toast, or crispy whole-wheat rolls.

SERVES 4

SCALLOPS IN SAFFRON SAUCE

Saffron is about the most expensive of all spices, but take
heart – only a few strands are needed in any recipe!

16 large scallops with coral attached
½ cup water
½ cup dry white wine
1 shallot, roughly chopped
1 bouquet garni, consisting of 1 bay leaf, 1 sprig of fresh
　　thyme and 3 stalks of parsley
6 black peppercorns
A few strands of saffron
4 tbsps hot water
1¼ cups heavy cream
3 tbsps fresh chopped parsley
Salt and pepper

1. Put the scallops into a large shallow pan together with
the water, wine, shallot, bouquet garni and peppercorns.

2. Cover the pan and bring the liquid almost to the boil.
Remove the pan from the heat and leave the scallops to
poach in the hot liquid for 10-15 minutes.

3. The scallops are cooked when they are just firm to the
touch. Remove them from the liquid and keep warm on a
clean plate.

4. Strain the scallop cooking liquid in a small saucepan
and bring to the boil. Allow the liquid to boil rapidly until it is
reduced by about half.

5. Soak the saffron in the hot water for about 5 minutes, or
until the color has infused into the water.

6. Add the saffron with its soaking liquid, the heavy cream
and the chopped parsley to the reduced cooking liquid
and season to taste. Bring the sauce back to just below
boiling point.

7. Arrange the scallops on a serving plate and pour a little
of the sauce over them before serving.

Step 4 Reduce
the cooking liquid
by half by boiling
rapidly over a high
heat.

Step 1 Put the
scallops into a
large shallow pan,
along with the
water, wine,
shallot, bouquet
garni and
peppercorns.

Step 5 Soak the
saffron in the hot
water for about 5
minutes, or until
the colour has
infused into the
water.

Cook's Notes

Time
Preparation takes about 15
minutes, and cooking also
takes about 15 minutes.

Preparation
If you do not wish to use
shellfish on the day you buy it,
it should be wrapped in newspaper and
stored in the bottom of the refrigerator
until the next day. It should not be kept
longer than overnight.

Serving Ideas
Serve as a starter with brown
bread and butter, or as a light
main course with rice or pasta.

SERVES 4

SHRIMP IN MELON

Deliciously cool and refreshing for a summer lunch, this recipe could also be served as an unusual appetizer for eight people.

2 small melons
4 medium tomatoes
1 small cucumber
1 orange
Juice of half a lemon
4 tbsps light vegetable oil
3 tbsps heavy cream
2 tbsps chopped fresh mint, reserve 4 sprigs for garnish
Pinch of sugar
Salt and pepper
1 tsp chopped fresh lemon thyme, optional
1¼ cups peeled shrimp
¾ cup toasted slivered almonds

Step 2 Prepare the fruit and vegetables so they are a convenient size to eat.

Step 3 Mix the dressing in a large bowl and add the rest of the ingredients to it, stirring well to coat thoroughly.

Step 1 Leave a ¼-inch border of flesh on the inside of each shell, so they are rigid enough to hold the salad.

1. Cut the melons in half through the middle, remove the seeds and scoop out the flesh with a melon baller, or spoon. Leave a ¼-inch border of fruit on the inside of each shell.

2. Cut the melon flesh into ½-inch cubes, or leave in balls. Peel the tomatoes and remove the seeds. Cut the flesh into

strips. Peel the cucumber, cut into half lengthways and then into ½-inch cubes. Peel and segment the orange.

3. In a large bowl, mix together the lemon juice, oil and heavy cream. Stir in the mint, sugar, salt and pepper and thyme, if using. Add the shrimp and the fruit and vegetables, and mix thoroughly to coat evenly with the dressing.

4. Pile equal quantities of fruit and shrimp mixture into the two shells and chill well.

5. Serve garnished with the reserved mint sprigs and the almonds.

Cook's Notes

Time
Preparation takes about 25 minutes. Allow at least 2 hours for chilling the salad, before serving.

Preparation
If the melon shells will not stand upright, cut a thin slice off the bottom of each one to make them more stable.

Serving Ideas
Serve with a mixed green salad and new potatoes.

Chapter II

SALADS

SERVES 4-6

CAESAR SALAD

Both Los Angeles and Tijuana take credit
for this salad, said to have been concocted one
evening from the only ingredients left in the kitchen.

6 anchovy fillets, soaked in 4 tbsps milk
1 cup olive oil
1 clove garlic, left whole
4 slices French bread, cut into ½″ cubes
1 egg, cooked 1 minute
1 head Romaine lettuce
Juice of 1 small lemon
Salt and pepper
4 tbsps grated Parmesan cheese

paper towels.

3. Break the cooked egg into a bowl and beat well with the lemon juice, salt and pepper. Toss the lettuce with the remaining garlic oil and anchovies. Add the egg mixture and toss to coat well. Place in a clean serving bowl and sprinkle over the croûtons and Parmesan cheese. Serve at room temperature.

Step 2 Fry the cubes of French bread in the hot oil, stirring them constantly for even browning.

Step 3 To make the dressing, break the egg into the bowl and mix well with the lemon juice and seasoning until slightly thickened.

1. Leave the anchovies to soak in the milk for 15 minutes. Rinse and pat dry on paper towels. Chop roughly.

2. Crush the garlic and leave in the oil for about 30 minutes. Heat all but 6 tbsps of the oil in a frying pan until hot. Fry the cubes of bread until golden brown, stirring constantly with a metal spoon for even browning. Drain on

Step 3 Add the oil to the lettuce separately and then toss with the egg dressing mixture.

Cook's Notes

Time
Preparation takes about 30 minutes and cooking takes about 3-5 minutes for the croûtons.

Cook's Tip
Soaking anchovy fillets in milk before using them neutralizes the strong salty taste.

Watchpoint
Remove the croûtons from the hot fat when just barely brown enough. They continue to cook slightly in their own heat as they drain.

SERVES 4-6

CHINA BEACH SALAD

Named for a stretch of beach near San Francisco,
this recipe reflects the Chinese heritage in California's
past and its present passion for salads.

1lb cooked, peeled shrimp
1lb seedless white grapes, halved if large
6 sticks celery, thinly sliced on diagonal
4oz toasted flaked almonds
4oz canned water chestnuts, sliced or diced
8oz canned lichees or 12oz fresh litchis, peeled
1 small fresh pineapple, peeled, cored and cut into
  pieces
1½ cups mayonnaise
1 tbsp honey
1 tbsp light soy sauce
2 tbps mild curry powder
Juice of half a lime
Chinese cabbage or Belgian endive (chicory)

Step 1 Trim the point of each quarter of pineapple to remove the core.

1. Combine the shrimp, grapes, celery, almonds, water chestnuts and litchis in a large bowl. Trim off the top and bottom of the pineapple and quarter. Slice off the points of each quarter to remove the core.

Step 2 Use a serrated fruit knife to slice between the skin and pineapple flesh.

2. Slice the pineapple skin away and cut the flesh into bite-size pieces. Add to the shrimp and toss to mix.

3. Break the Chinese cabbage or endive and wash them well. If using Chinese cabbage, shred the leafy part finely, saving the thicker ends of the leaves for other use. Place the Chinese cabbage on salad plates. Mix the remaining dressing ingredients thoroughly. Pile the salad ingredients onto the leaves and spoon over some of the dressing, leaving the ingredients showing. Separate chicory leaves and arrange them whole. Serve remaining dressing separately.

Step 2 Add pineapple pieces to the shrimp and mix well.

Cook's Notes

 Time
Preparation takes about 30 minutes.

 Serving Ideas
Serve as a main course salad for lunch or a light dinner. Serve in smaller quantities as an appetizer.

Variation
Other seafood may be substituted for the shrimp. Use crab, lobster or shellfish such as mussels.

SERVES 4

SHRIMP REMOULADE

The shrimp in this dish 'cook' in the refrigerator in a marinade
that is piquant with mustard, horseradish and wine vinegar.

1½lbs raw unshelled large shrimp
3 tbsps mild mustard
2 tsps horseradish
1 tbsp paprika
1 fresh chili pepper, seeded and finely chopped
1 clove garlic, crushed
Salt
½ cup white wine vinegar
1½ cups oil
6 green onions, sliced
2 sticks celery, thinly sliced
2 bay leaves
2 tbsps chopped parsley
Lettuce and lemon wedges

Step 2 Combine marinade ingredients in a bowl and stir in the vinegar.

Step 3 Using a small whisk, gradually whisk in the oil until the sauce is smooth and thick.

1. Shell the shrimp, except for the very tail ends. If desired, the shrimp may be completely shelled.

2. Combine the mustard, horseradish, paprika, chili pepper, garlic and salt in a deep bowl. Mix in the vinegar thoroughly.

3. Add the oil in a thin, steady stream while beating constantly with a small whisk. Continue to beat until the sauce is smooth and thick. Add the green onions, celery, bay leaves and chopped parsley. Cover the bowl tightly and leave in the refrigerator for several hours, or overnight.

4. Two hours before serving, add the shrimp to the marinade and stir to coat them well. Leave in the refrigerator until ready to serve.

5. To serve, shred the lettuce finely and place on individual serving plates. Arrange the shrimp on top and spoon over some of the marinade to serve, discarding the bay leaves.

Step 4 Add the shrimp to the marinade and stir well to coat.

Cook's Notes

Time
Preparation takes about 25 minutes plus overnight chilling for the marinade and 2 hours marinating time for the shrimp.

Cook's Tip
After two hours' marinating, the seafood will look cooked, that is opaque and slightly firm. However, it is still raw, so absolutely fresh seafood is required.

Variation
Scallops, quartered or sliced, depending on the size, mussels, clams or whitefish, cut into thin strips, may be used instead of or in addition to the shrimp.

SERVES 4

CRAB LOUIS

This salad is legendary on Fisherman's Wharf in San Francisco. Once tasted, it is sure to become a favorite.

2 large cooked crabs
1 head iceberg lettuce
4 large tomatoes
4 hard-cooked eggs
16 black olives
1 cup prepared mayonnaise
4 tbsps whipping cream
4 tbsps chili sauce or tomato chutney
½ green pepper, seeded and finely diced
3 green onions, finely chopped
Salt and pepper

1. To prepare the crabs, break off the claws and set them aside. Turn the crabs over and press up with thumbs to separate the body from the shell of each.

2. Cut the body into quarters and use a skewer to pick out the white meat. Discard the stomach sac and lungs (deadman's fingers). Scrape out the brown meat from the shell to use, if desired.

3. Crack the large claws and legs and remove the meat. Break into shreds, discarding any shell or cartilage.

Combine all the meat and set it aside.

4. Shred the lettuce finely, quarter the tomatoes and chop the eggs.

5. Combine the mayonnaise, cream, chili sauce or chutney, green pepper and green onions and mix well.

6. Arrange the shredded lettuce on serving plates and divide the crab meat evenly.

7. Spoon some of the dressing over each serving of crab and sprinkle with the chopped egg. Garnish each serving with tomato wedges and olives and serve the remaining dressings separately.

Step 1 Turn crabs over and press up with thumbs to separate the under-body from the shell.

Cook's Notes

Time
Preparation takes about 30-40 minutes.

Preparation
To shred lettuce finely, break off the leaves and stack them up a few at a time. Use a large, sharp knife to cut across the leaves into thin shreds.

Variation
Frozen crab meat may be used instead of fresh. Make sure it is completely defrosted and well drained before using. Pick through the meat to remove any bits of shell or cartilage left behind.

SERVES 4

RED SNAPPER NIÇOISE

Red snapper is now widely available and its attractive appearance lends itself to this colorful dish.

2 tbsps red wine vinegar
8 tbsps olive oil
¼ tsp French mustard
Handful of chopped fresh mixed herbs
1 shallot, finely chopped
1 clove garlic, crushed
Salt and pepper
1 cup button mushrooms, quartered
4 red snapper, descaled and cleaned
Seasoned flour
Lemon juice
1lb tomatoes, quartered and cores removed
1 green pepper, seeded and sliced
¼ cup pitted black olives, halved
2 hard cooked eggs, quartered
Small can anchovy fillets

Step 2 Put the mushrooms into a bowl with the dressing and stir to coat them evenly.

Step 3 Toss the snapper in just enough seasoned flour to coat lightly, before cooking.

1. In a screw top jar, shake together the vinegar, 6 tablespoons of the olive oil, the mustard, herbs, shallot, garlic and seasoning, to make a French dressing.

2. Put the mushrooms into a bowl and pour over the French dressing. Stir to coat the mushrooms evenly and refrigerate for about 1 hour.

3. Toss the snapper in the seasoned flour to coat lightly. Heat the remaining oil in a frying pan and fry the fish on both sides for 2-3 minutes per side, taking care not to break the fish. Sprinkle lightly with lemon juice and salt and

pepper, and allow to go cold.

4. When ready to serve, add the tomatoes, pepper, olives and eggs to the mushrooms. Stir together gently, to coat the salad with the dressing.

5. Pile the salad onto a serving dish and arrange the red snapper on top. Garnish with the drained anchovy fillets.

Cook's Notes

Time
Preparation takes about 15 minutes. Cooking takes about 15 minutes.

Cook's Tip
The French dressing is delicious with other salads, so make extra. It will keep in a screw top jar in the refrigerator for up to 2 weeks.

Serving Ideas
Serve with hot French bread or crusty rolls.

SERVES 4

SEVICHE

Do not be put off by the thought of eating raw fish, as the cod will "cook" in the spicy marinade and the result is absolutely delicious.

1lb cod fillets
Juice and grated rind of 2 limes
1 shallot, chopped
1 green chili pepper, seeded and finely chopped
1 tsp ground coriander
1 small green pepper, seeded and sliced
1 small red pepper, seeded and sliced
1 tbsp chopped fresh parsley
1 tbsp chopped fresh coriander leaves
4 green olives, chopped
2 tbsps olive oil
Salt and pepper
1 small lettuce

Step 2 Stir the lime juice and rind, together with the shallot and spices, into the strips of cod, mixing thoroughly to coat them evenly with the spice mixture.

Step 4 Stir the peppers, herbs, onion and oil into the drained fish.

Step 1 Cut the skinned cod fillets into thin strips across the grain, removing any bones you may find.

1. Skin the cod fillets and cut them into thin strips across the grain.

2. Put the cod strips into a bowl, pour over the lime juice and rind. Add the shallot, chili pepper and coriander, and stir well to coat the fish completely.

3. Cover the bowl and refrigerate for 24 hours, stirring occasionally.

4. When ready to serve, drain the fish and stir in the peppers, parsley, coriander leaves, onions and oil. Season to taste and serve on a bed of lettuce.

Cook's Notes

 Time
Preparation takes about 20 minutes, plus 24 hours refrigeration.

 Variation
Substitute haddock or monkfish fillets for the cod.

 Serving Ideas
Serve with crusty French bread or tortilla chips.

SERVES 4

SHRIMP AND CASHEWS IN PINEAPPLE WITH TARRAGON DRESSING

Served in the pineapple shells, this impressive salad is ideal
for a summer lunch or buffet.

2 small fresh pineapples, with nice green tops
1¼ cups cooked, peeled shrimp
1 cup roasted, unsalted cashew nuts
2 sticks of celery, thinly sliced
4 tbsps lemon juice
1 egg
2 tbsps superfine sugar
1 tbsp tarragon vinegar
2 tsps chopped fresh tarragon
½ cup whipping cream

Step 1 Cut the pineapples in half lengthways, making sure that the leafy tops stay intact.

1. Cut the pineapples carefully in half lengthways, leaving their green tops attached.

2. Cut out the pineapple flesh carefully, leaving a ¼-inch border of flesh on the inside of the shell. Remove the cores and cut the flesh into bite-sized pieces.

3. Put the chopped pineapple into a bowl, along with the shrimp, cashew nuts and celery. Pour in the lemon juice and mix well. Divide the mixture equally between the pineapple shells, and chill them in the refrigerator.

4. In a heat-proof bowl, whisk together the egg and sugar. Stand the bowl over a pan of simmering water, and whisk in the vinegar and tarragon. Continue whisking until the mixture has thickened.

5. Remove the bowl from the heat and allow to cool completely, whisking occasionally.

6. When completely cold, whip the cream until it is just beginning to thicken, then fold it into the dressing mixture.

7. Pour the cream dressing over the salad in the pineapple shells and serve.

Step 4 Whisk the egg and sugar mixture, together with the vinegar and the tarragon, over a pan of simmering water, until it is pale and thick.

Step 6 Fold the lightly whipped cream carefully into the tarragon and egg dressing, before pouring it over the individual salads.

Cook's Notes

Time
Preparation takes about 30 minutes, and cooking about 10–15 minutes.

Preparation
Whisking the egg and sugar dressing can be done with an electric mixer. It will not then be necessary to whisk the dressing over a pan of hot water.

Cook's Tip
If you cannot buy unsalted cashew nuts, wash salted ones in water, but make sure they are completely dry before adding them to the salad.

SERVES 4

VINEGARED CRAB

An unusual way of serving fresh crab. You should be able to
buy the rice vinegar from a delicatessen or health food
shop. If not, substitute white wine vinegar.

1 small cucumber, grated
Salt, for sprinkling
1 large cooked crab
1 small piece fresh ginger, grated
Chinese cabbage, for serving
3 tbsps rice vinegar
2 tbsps dry sherry
2 tbsps soy sauce

1. Sprinkle the cucumber with salt and leave for 30 minutes.

2. Crack the legs and claws off the crab. Remove the meat from the claws and legs, but leave four thin legs whole as a garnish.

3. Separate the underbody from the shell. Remove and discard the stomach sac and the gray, feathered gills.

4. Scrape the brown meat from the shell and crack open the underbody. Use a skewer to pick out the meat.

5. Rinse the cucumber, drain well and squeeze out excess moisture. Mix together the cucumber, crab meat and ginger.

6. Arrange the Chinese cabbage on serving plates, to represent crab shells. Pile equal quantities of crab mixture onto the Chinese cabbage, leaving some of the leaf showing. Garnish with a whole crab leg and some grated, pickled ginger, if you can get it.

7. Mix together the vinegar, sherry and soy sauce. Serve with the crab in little bowls.

Step 2 Remove meat from claws and legs.

Step 4 Crack open the underbody of the crab and use a skewer to remove the white meat inside.

Cook's Notes

Time
Preparation takes about 30 minutes.

Cook's Tip
When choosing a fresh crab, select one which feels heavy for its size and inside which, when shaken, no water can be heard.

Serving Ideas
A rice or pasta salad would be excellent with this dish.

Chapter III

EVERYDAY DISHES

SERVES 2

BARBECUED SHRIMP

It's the sauce rather than the cooking method that
gives this dish its name. It's spicy, zippy and *hot*.

1lb large shrimp, cooked and unpeeled
½ cup unsalted butter
1 tsp each white, black and cayenne pepper
Pinch salt
1 tsp each chopped fresh thyme, rosemary and
  marjoram
1 clove garlic, crushed
1 tsp Worcester sauce
½ cup fish stock
4 tbsps dry white wine
Cooked rice

Remove the shrimp and set them aside.

3. Add the Worcester sauce, stock and wine to the ingredients in the pan. Bring to the boil and cook for about 3 minutes to reduce. Add salt to taste.

4. Arrange the shrimp on a bed of rice and pour over the sauce to serve.

Step 1 Remove the legs and eyes from the shrimp. Leave on the long antennae, if desired.

Step 2 Melt the butter and add the spices and herbs and shrimp, and cook briefly.

Step 3 Add the Worcester sauce, wine and stock to the pan and boil rapidly to reduce.

1. Remove the eyes and the legs from the shrimp.

2. Melt the butter in a large frying pan and add the white pepper, black pepper, cayenne pepper, herbs and garlic. Add the shrimp and toss over heat for a few minutes.

Cook's Notes

 Time
Preparation takes about 15 minutes and cooking takes about 5 minutes.

Preparation
Because the shrimp are pre-cooked, cook them very briefly again, just to heat through. Use uncooked, unpeeled shrimp if possible. Cook these until they curl and turn pink.

 Serving Ideas
The shrimp may also be served cold. If serving cold, prepare the sauce with 6 tbsps oil instead of the butter.

SERVES 6

SEAFOOD STEW

This makes the most of the delicious
and varied fish and shellfish found
off Spain's beautiful coastline.

24 clams or mussels in the shell
3 squid
2lb firm whitefish, filleted into 2 inch pieces
3 medium-sized tomatoes, peeled, seeded and chopped
½ green pepper, seeded and chopped
1 small onion, chopped
1 clove garlic, finely chopped
1 cup dry white wine
Salt and pepper
½ cup olive oil
6 slices French bread
3 tbsps chopped parsley

1. Scrub the clams or mussels well to remove the beards and barnacles. Discard any shellfish with broken shells or ones that do not close when tapped. Place the mussels or clams in a large saucepan or heatproof casserole, scatter over about half of the vegetables and garlic and spoon over 4 tbsps of the olive oil.

2. To clean the squid, hold the tail section in one hand and the head section in the other to pull the tail away from the head.

3. Cut the tentacles free from the head just above the eyes. Discard the head, entrails and ink sack.

4. Remove the quill from the body of the squid and peel away the reddish-purple outer skin.

5. Slice the tail into strips about ½ inch thick. Cut the tentacles into individual pieces.

6. Scatter the squid and the prepared whitefish over the vegetables in the pan and top with the remaining vegetables. Pour over the white wine and season with salt and pepper. Bring to the boil over high heat and then reduce to simmering. Cover the pan and cook for about 20 minutes or until the clams open, the squid is tender and the fish flakes easily. Discard any clams or mussels that do not open.

7. Heat the remaining olive oil in a frying pan and when hot, add the slices of bread, browning them well on both sides. Drain on paper towels.

8. Place a slice of bread in the bottom of a soup bowl and ladle the fish mixture over the bread. Sprinkle with parsley and serve immediately.

Step 2
To clean the squid, separate the head from the tail by pulling them in opposite directions

Step 4
Remove the quill from the tail and peel the reddish-purple skin from the outside.

 Cook's Notes

Time
Preparation takes about 35 minutes and cooking takes about 20 minutes.

Preparation
Fry the bread while the fish stew is cooking. The stew must be served immediately and not reheated.

Variation
Different kinds of fish, such as haddock, cod, halibut or sea bass can be used.

SERVES 4

PLAICE WITH SPICY TOMATO SAUCE

This piquant fish dish is popular along
Mexico's Gulf coast.

3oz cream cheese
1 tsp dried oregano
Pinch cayenne pepper
4 whole fillets of plaice
Lime slices and dill to garnish

Tomato Sauce

1 tbsp oil
1 small onion, chopped
1 stick celery, chopped
1 chili pepper, seeded and chopped
¼ tsp each ground cumin, coriander and ginger
½ red and ½ green pepper, seeded and chopped
14oz canned tomatoes
1 tbsp tomato paste
Salt, pepper and a pinch sugar

1. Heat the oil in a heavy-based pan and cook the onion, celery, chili pepper and spices for about 5 minutes over very low heat.

2. Add red and green peppers and the remaining ingredients and bring to the boil. Reduce heat and simmer 15-20 minutes, stirring occasionally. Set aside while preparing the fish.

3. Mix the cream cheese, oregano and cayenne pepper together and set aside.

4. Skin the fillets using a filleting knife. Start at the tail end and hold the knife at a slight angle to the skin.

5. Push the knife along using a sawing motion, with the blade against the skin. Dip fingers in salt to make it easier to hold onto the fish skin. Gradually separate the fish from the skin.

6. Spread the cheese filling on all 4 fillets and roll each up. Secure with wooden picks.

7. Place the fillets in a lightly greased baking dish, cover and cook for 10 minutes in a preheated 350°F oven.

8. Pour over the tomato sauce and cook a further 10-15 minutes. Fish is cooked when it feels firm and looks opaque. Garnish with lime slices and dill.

Step 5 Using a filleting knife held at an angle, push the knife along, cutting against the fish skin. Use a sawing motion to separate flesh from skin.

Step 6 Spread cheese filling on the fish and roll up each fillet.

Cook's Notes

Time
Preparation takes about 30 minutes and cooking takes 20-25 minutes.

Serving Ideas
Add rice and an avocado salad.

Special Occasions
Add shrimp or crabmeat to the filling for a dinner party dish.

SERVES 6

CHILI SHRIMP QUICHE

Fresh chili peppers give a Mexican flavor
to this quiche with its shrimp filling.

Pastry

1 cup all-purpose flour
Pinch salt
2 tbsps butter or margarine
2 tbsps white cooking fat
2-4 tbsps cold water

Filling

4 eggs
½ cup milk
½ cup light cream
½ clove garlic, crushed
1 cup Cheddar cheese, grated
3 green onions, chopped
2 green chilies, seeded and chopped
8oz cooked and peeled shrimp
Salt
Cooked, unpeeled shrimp and parsley sprigs for garnish

1. Sift the flour with a pinch of salt into a mixing bowl, or place in a food processor and mix once or twice.

2. Rub in the butter and fat until the mixture resembles fine breadcrumbs, or work in the food processor, being careful not to over-mix.

3. Mix in the liquid gradually, adding enough to bring the pastry together into a ball. In a food processor, add the liquid through the funnel while the machine is running.

4. Wrap the pastry well and chill for 20-30 minutes.

5. Roll out the pastry on a well-floured surface with a floured rolling pin.

6. Wrap the circle of pastry around the rolling pin to lift it into a 10 inch flan dish. Unroll the pastry over the dish.

7. Carefully press the pastry onto the bottom and up the sides of the dish, taking care not to stretch it.

8. Roll the rolling pin over the top of the dish to remove excess pastry, or cut off with a sharp knife.

9. Mix the eggs, milk, cream and garlic together. Sprinkle the cheese, onion, chilies and shrimp onto the base of the pastry and pour over the egg mixture.

10. Bake in a preheated 400°F oven for 30-40 minutes until firm and golden brown. Peel the tail shells off the shrimp and remove the legs and roe if present. Use to garnish the quiche along with the sprigs of parsley.

Step 6 Use the rolling pin to help lift the pastry into the flan dish.

Step 7 Carefully press the pastry into the dish to line the base and sides.

Cook's Notes

 Time
Preparation takes about 40 minutes, which includes time for the pastry to chill. Cooking takes 30-40 minutes.

 Variation
Add diced red or green peppers and chopped coriander leaves to the filling before baking.

 Serving Ideas
Serve as a starter, cut in thin wedges or baked in individual dishes. Serve hot or cold with a salad for a snack or light meal.

SERVES 4-6

BOATMAN'S STEW

This quick, economical and satisfying
fish dish will please any fish lover
for lunch or a light supper.

6 tbsps olive oil
2 large onions, sliced
1 red pepper, seeded and sliced
4oz mushrooms, sliced
1lb canned tomatoes
Pinch salt and pepper
Pinch dried thyme
1½ cups water
2lb whitefish fillets, skinned
½ cup white wine
2 tbsps chopped parsley

1. Heat the oil in a large saucepan and add the onions. Cook until beginning to look translucent. Add the pepper and cook until the vegetables are softened.

2. Add the mushrooms and the tomatoes and bring the mixture to the boil.

3. Add thyme, salt, pepper and water and simmer for about 30 minutes.

4. Add the fish and wine and cook until the fish flakes easily, about 15 minutes. Stir in parsley.

5. To serve, place a piece of toasted French bread in the bottom of the soup bowl and spoon over the fish stew.

Use a sharp knife to cut the onion into thin crosswise slices.

Step 1 Cook the onions in the oil along with the peppers until soft.

Cook's Notes

Time
Preparation takes about 20 minutes and cooking takes about 45 minutes.

Variation
Shellfish may be added with the fish, if desired. Substitute green peppers for red peppers.

Serving Ideas
The stew may also be served over rice. Accompany with a green salad.

SERVES 4

BROILED FLOUNDER

A mayonnaise-like topping puffs
to a golden brown to give this mild-
flavored fish a piquant taste.

4 double fillets of flounder
2 eggs, separated
Pinch salt, pepper and dry mustard
1 cup peanut oil
4 tbsps pickle relish
1 tbsp chopped parsley
1 tbsp lemon juice
Dash tabasco

1. Place the egg yolks in a blender, food processor or deep bowl.

2. Blend in the salt, pepper and mustard. If blending by hand, use a small whisk.

3. If using the machine, pour the oil through the funnel in a thin, steady stream with the machine running. If mixing by hand, add oil a few drops at a time, beating well in between each addition.

4. When half the oil has been added, the rest may be added in a thin steady stream while beating constantly with a small whisk.

5. Mix in the relish, parsley, lemon juice and tabasco. Beat the egg whites until stiff but not dry and fold into the mayonnaise.

6. Broil the fish about 2 inches from the heat source for about 6-10 minutes, depending on the thickness of the fillets.

7. Spread the sauce over each fillet and broil for 3-5 minutes longer, or until the sauce puffs and browns lightly.

Step 4 Add the oil to the egg yolk mixture in a thin, steady stream while beating constantly.

Step 5 Fold stiffly-beaten egg whites thoroughly into the mayonnaise.

Step 7 Spread or spoon the sauce over each fish fillet before broiling.

Cook's Notes

Time
Preparation takes about 20 minutes. If preparing the mayonnaise by hand this will take about 15-20 minutes. The fish takes 9-15 minutes to cook.

Watchpoint
When preparing the mayonnaise either by machine or by hand, do not add the oil too quickly or the mayonnaise will curdle. If it does curdle, beat another egg yolk in a bowl and gradually beat in the curdled mixture. This should bring it back together again.

Variation
This same topping may be used on other fish besides flounder.

Serving Ideas
Serve with broiled tomatoes.

SERVES 4

FISH, ZUCCHINI AND LEMON KEBABS

Rolled fish looks elegant and makes a dish that is slightly
out of the ordinary.

16 small, thin sole fillets, or 8 larger ones, skinned and
   cut in half lengthways
4 tbsps olive oil
1 clove garlic, crushed
Juice ½ lemon
Finely grated rind ½ lemon
Freshly ground sea salt and black pepper, to taste
3 drops Tabasco sauce
2 medium-sized zucchini, cut into ¼-inch slices
1 green pepper, halved, seeded and cut into 1-inch
   pieces

1. Roll up each sole fillet like a jelly roll and secure with a
wooden pick.

Step 1 Roll up each sole fillet like a jelly roll, from a narrow end, and secure each roll with a wooden pick.

2. Place the fish rolls in a shallow dish. Mix together the olive oil, garlic, lemon juice, lemon rind, salt and pepper and Tabasco sauce.

3. Spoon the olive oil mixture evenly over fish rolls, and chill for about 2 hours.

4. Remove the wooden picks, and carefully thread the rolled fish fillets onto kebab skewers alternately with the zucchini slices and pieces of green pepper.

5. Brush each threaded kebab with a little of the lemon and oil marinade.

6. Arrange the kebab skewers on a broiler pan and cook under a moderately hot broiler for about 8 minutes, carefully turning the kebabs once or twice during cooking and brushing them with a little of the remaining marinade, if required.

Step 4 Thread the rolled fish onto kebab skewers alternately with a zucchini slices and pieces of green pepper.

Cook's Notes

Time
Preparation takes about 30 minutes, plus 2 hours chilling time, and cooking takes about 8 minutes.

Cook's Tip
The marinade ingredients are delicious used with other types of fish.

Variation
If sole is not in season, substitute small dab or plaice.

Serving Ideas
Serve the kebabs on a bed of brown rice, sprinkled with chopped parsley.

SERVES 4

COD IN PAPRIKA SAUCE

Creamy paprika sauce complements the flavor of cod
magnificently in this tasty recipe.

1lb cod fillets
Lemon juice
1 bay leaf
Slice of onion
6 peppercorns
2 tbsps butter
½ cup button mushrooms, trimmed and sliced
1 small red pepper, seeded and sliced
1 shallot, finely chopped
2 tsps paprika pepper
1 clove garlic, crushed
¼ cup all-purpose flour
1 cup milk
1 tbsp chopped fresh parsley
1 tsp chopped fresh thyme
1 tsp tomato paste
Salt and pepper
8oz fresh pasta, cooked
2 tbsps sour cream, or natural yogurt

Step 4 Stir just enough of the strained fish liquor into the sauce for it to coat the back of a spoon.

Step 1 Put the cod chunks into an ovenproof dish, along with the bay leaf, lemon juice, onion slice and peppercorns. Pour in just enough water to cover the fish.

1. Cut the fish into 1-inch chunks. Put these into an ovenproof dish with the lemon juice, bay leaf, onion, peppercorns and just enough water to cover. Cover with a lid and poach for about 10 minutes in a preheated oven, 350°F.

2. Melt the butter in a saucepan and stir in the mushrooms, pepper, shallot, paprika and garlic. Cook gently, until the pepper begins to soften.

3. Stir the flour into the mushrooms and peppers. Gradually add the milk, stirring until the sauce has thickened.

4. Remove the fish from the dish and strain off the liquor. Stir enough of this liquor into the pepper sauce to make it of coating consistency. Add the parsley, thyme and tomato paste to the sauce and simmer for 2-3 minutes. Season to taste.

5. Arrange the hot, cooked pasta on a serving plate and place the cod on top. Coat with the paprika sauce, and spoon over the sour cream, or yogurt, to serve.

Cook's Notes

Time
Preparation takes about 20 minutes, and cooking takes about 16 minutes.

Variation
Use any other firm-fleshed whitefish, e.g. monkfish, instead of the cod.

Serving Ideas
A mixed salad would be ideal to serve with this dish.

SERVES 4

BROILED HERRINGS WITH DILL AND MUSTARD

Dill and mustard give herring a delicious tangy flavor.

4 tbsps chopped fresh dill
6 tbsps mild Swedish mustard
2 tbsps lemon juice, or white wine
4-8 fresh herrings, cleaned but heads and tails left on
2 tbsps butter or margarine, melted
Salt and pepper

Step 1 In a small bowl mix the dill, mustard and lemon juice, or white wine, together thoroughly.

1. Mix the dill, mustard and lemon juice, or wine, together thoroughly.

2. Cut three slits, just piercing the skin, on both sides of each herring and lay them on a broiler pan.

3. Spread half the mustard mixture equally over the exposed side of each fish, pushing some into the cuts.

4. Spoon a little of the melted butter over each herring, and broil the fish for 5-6 minutes.

5. Turn the fish over and spread the remaining mustard and dill mixture over them. Spoon over the remaining melted butter and broil for a further 5-6 minutes.

6. Sprinkle the fish with a little salt and pepper before serving.

Step 2 Cut three slits, just piercing the skin, on both sides of each fish. Take care not to cut the fish too deeply, or the flesh may break when it is turned over.

Step 3 Spread half the mustard mixture equally over the top side of each fish, pushing some of the mixture gently into each cut.

Cook's Notes

Time
Preparation takes about 10 minutes, and cooking takes 12-15 minutes, although this may be longer if the herring are large.

Variation
Use whole fresh mackerel in place of the herring.

Serving Ideas
Arrange the fish on a serving dish, garnished with lemon wedges and sprigs of fresh dill. Serve with new potatoes, if available.

SERVES 4

SHRIMP CRESPELLE

A delicious dish from Italy, crespelle are simply rich, wafer-thin pancakes.

3 eggs, beaten
¾ cup all-purpose flour
Salt
1 cup water
1 tsp olive oil
3 tbsps butter or margarine, melted
2 tbsps butter
2 tsps all-purpose flour
1½ cups milk
Juice 1 lemon
Salt and pepper
1¼ cups shrimp
Lemon slices, to garnish

1. Sift the ¾ cup flour into a bowl, whisk the eggs into the flour gradually, until the mixture is smooth. Stir in the water and oil and leave the batter to stand for 30 minutes.

2. Heat a frying pan and brush it lightly with the melted butter. Put 1 tablespoon of the batter in the center and roll and tilt the pan to coat the base evenly.

3. Fry until the pancake is golden brown underneath, then carefully turn over, to brown the other side. Stack and keep warm until required. Repeat until all the batter has been used up.

4. Melt the 2 tbsps of butter in a saucepan and stir in the 2 tablespoons of flour. Gradually add the milk, beating well, and returning the pan to the heat between additions, until all the milk has been incorporated. Simmer the sauce for 2-3 minutes. Stir in the lemon juice and season to taste.

5. Mix together half of the sauce and the shrimp. Put one pancake into an ovenproof dish and spread a spoonful of the shrimp sauce over this. Cover with another pancake and repeat the sauce/pancake procedure until all the pancakes have been used up, finishing with a pancake. Bake in a preheated oven, 375°F, for 10 minutes.

6. Cover with the remaining sauce and garnish with lemon slices. Cut the crespelle like a cake, to serve.

Step 2 Heat and lightly grease a 7-inch frying pan. Put 1 tablespoon of batter into the center and roll and tilt the pan, to coat the base evenly with the batter.

Step 5 Put alternate layers of pancake and sauce into an ovenproof dish. Finish with a pancake and bake.

Cook's Notes

Time
Preparation takes about 40 minutes. Cooking takes about 30 minutes.

Serving Ideas
Serve this dish with a colorful mixed salad.

Freezing
Pancakes can be made in advance and frozen in stacks, with a piece of wax paper between each one. To use, allow the pancakes to defrost, then reheat as required.

SERVES 4

PROVENÇALE FISH STEW

A hearty Mediterranean lunch or dinner, this dish is a real
delight for fish lovers.

1 medium onion, finely chopped
2 cloves garlic, crushed
3 tbsps olive oil
1½lbs tomatoes, skinned, seeded and chopped
2 cups dry red wine
2 tbsps tomato paste
Salt and pepper
4 cups fresh mussels in their shells, scrubbed and
    debearded
8 large Mediterranean shrimp
¾ cup peeled shrimp
4 crab claws, shelled but with the claw tips left intact

Step 3 Cook the musseis in the tomato sauce, until all the shells have opened.

Step 1 Gently fry the tomatoes with the onions and garlic, until they are beginning to soften.

1. In a large pan, fry the onion and garlic together gently in the olive oil, until they are soft but not brown. Add the tomatoes and fry until they begin to soften.

2. Stir in the red wine and the tomato paste. Season to taste, then bring to the boil, cover and simmer for about 15 minutes.

3. Add the mussels, re-cover the pan and simmer for 5-8 minutes, or until all the mussel shells are open. Discard any that remain closed.

4. Stir in the remaining ingredients and cook, uncovered, for about 5-8 minutes, or until the shell fish has thoroughly heated through.

Cook's Notes

Time
Preparation will take about 15 minutes, plus about 10 minutes for cleaning the mussels. Cooking takes about 35 minutes.

Serving Ideas
Deep-fry chunks of crusty bread, then sprinkle with garlic salt and parsley, to serve with the fish stew.

Preparation
To make sure the mussels are fresh, whilst scrubbing them, tap any open ones sharply with a knife. If they do not shut tight, quite quickly, discard them. Also discard any with broken shells or that do not open after cooking.

Cook's Tip
If you have to keep the mussels overnight, wrap them in damp newspaper and store them in the vegetable tray at the bottom of the refrigerator.

SERVES 6

PAELLA

This dish has as many variations as Spain
has cooks! Fish, meat and poultry combine with
vegetables and rice to make a complete meal.

12 mussels in their shells
6 clams (if not available use 6 more mussels)
6oz cod, skinned and cut into 2 inch pieces
12 large shrimp
3 chorizos or other spicy sausage
2lb chicken cut in 12 serving-size pieces
1 small onion, chopped
1 clove garlic, crushed
2 small peppers, red and green, seeded and shredded
1lb long grain rice
Large pinch saffron
Salt and pepper
4 cups boiling water
5oz frozen peas
3 tomatoes, peeled, seeded and chopped or shredded

1. Scrub the clams and mussels well to remove beards
and barnacles. Discard any with broken shells or those that
do not close when tapped. Leave the mussels and clams to
soak in water with a handful of flour for 30 minutes.

2. Remove the heads and legs from the shrimp, if desired,
but leave on the tail shells.

3. Place the sausage in a saucepan and cover with water.
Bring to the boil and then simmer for 5 minutes. Drain and
slice into ¼ inch rounds. Set aside.

4. Heat the oil and fry the chicken pieces, browning evenly
on both sides. Remove and drain on paper towels.

5. Add the sausage, onions, garlic and peppers to the oil in
the frying pan and fry briskly for about 3 minutes.

6. Combine the sausage mixture with uncooked rice and
saffron and place in a special Paella dish or a large oven-

and flame-proof casserole. Pour on the water, season with
salt and pepper and bring to the boil. Stir occasionally and
allow to boil for about 2 minutes.

7. Add the chicken pieces and place in a preheated 400°F
oven for about 15 minutes.

8. Add the clams, mussels, shrimp, cod and peas and
cook a further 10-15 minutes or until the rice is tender,
chicken is cooked and mussels and clams open. Discard
any that do not open. Add the tomatoes 5 minutes before
the end of cooking time and serve immediately.

Step 5
Cook the saus-
ages, onions
garlic and
peppers briefly in
oil.

Step 6
Combine the
sausage mixture,
rice and water in
a special Paella
dish or flame-
proof casserole.

Cook's Notes

 Time
Preparation takes about 30-40
minutes, cooking takes about
35-40 minutes.

 Variation
Vary the ingredients to suit
your own taste. Use other
kinds of fish and shellfish. Omit chicken
or substitute pork for part of the
quantity. Use red or green onions if
desired and add more sausage.

 Watchpoint
Do not stir the Paella once it
goes into the oven.

SERVES 4

RAIE AU BEURRE NOIR

It is amazing how the addition of simple ingredients like browned butter, vinegar, capers and parsley can turn an ordinary fish into a French masterpiece.

4 wings of skate
1 slice onion
2 parsley stalks
Pinch salt
6 black peppercorns

Beurre Noir

4 tbsps butter
2 tbsps white wine vinegar
1 tbsp capers
1 tbsp chopped parsley (optional)

1. Place the skate in one layer in a large, deep pan. Completely cover with water and add the onion, parsley stalks, salt and peppercorns. Bring gently to the boil with pan uncovered. Allow to simmer 15-20 minutes, or until the skate is done.

2. Lift the fish out onto a serving dish and remove the skin and any large pieces of bone. Take care not to break up the fish.

3. Place the butter in a small pan and cook over high heat until it begins to brown. Add the capers and immediately remove the butter from the heat. Add the vinegar, which will cause the butter to bubble. Add parsley, if using, and pour immediately over the fish to serve.

Step 1 Place the skate in a pan with the poaching liquid.

Step 2 Carefully remove any skin or large bones from the cooked fish, with a small knife.

Step 3 Pour sizzling butter over the fish to serve.

Cook's Notes

Variations
Chopped black olives, shallots or mushrooms may be used instead of or in addition to the capers. Add lemon juice instead of vinegar, if desired.

Cook's Tip
When the skate is done, it will pull away from the bones in long strips.

Time
Preparation takes about 20 minutes, cooking takes 15-20 minutes for the fish and about 5 minutes to brown the butter.

SERVES 4

FISH MILANESE

These fish, cooked in the style of
Milan, have a crispy crumb coating
and the fresh tang of lemon juice.

8 sole or plaice fillets
2 tbsps dry vermouth
1 bay leaf
6 tbsps olive oil
Salt and pepper
Seasoned flour for dredging
2 eggs, lightly beaten
Dry breadcrumbs
Oil for shallow frying
6 tbsps butter
1 clove garlic, crushed
2 tsps chopped parsley
2 tbsps capers
1 tsp chopped fresh oregano
Juice of 1 lemon
Salt and pepper
Lemon wedges and parsley to garnish

1. Skin the fillets with a sharp filleting knife. Remove any small bones and place the fillets in a large, shallow dish. Combine the vermouth, oil and bay leaf in a small saucepan and heat gently. Allow to cool completely and pour over the fish. Leave the fish to marinate for about 1 hour, turning them occasionally.

2. Remove the fish from the marinade and dredge lightly with the seasoned flour.

3. Dip the fillets into the beaten eggs to coat, or use a pastry brush to brush the eggs onto the fillets. Dip the egg-coated fillet into the breadcrumbs, pressing the crumbs on firmly.

4. Heat the oil in a large frying pan. Add the fillets and cook slowly on both sides until golden brown. Cook for about 3 minutes on each side, remove and drain on paper towels.

5. Pour the oil out of the frying pan and wipe it clean. Add the butter and the garlic and cook until both turn a light brown. Add the herbs, capers and lemon juice and pour immediately over the fish. Garnish with lemon wedges and sprigs of parsley.

Step 1 Hold each fillet firmly by the tail end and work a sharp filleting knife down the length of the fillet, holding the knife at a slight angle. Keep the blade as close as possible to the fish.

Step 3 Dip or brush the fillets with the beaten egg and press on the breadcrumb coating firmly.

Cook's Notes

Time
Preparation takes 1 hour for the fish to marinate, cooking takes about 6 minutes. It may be necessary to cook the fish in several batches, depending upon the size of the frying pan.

Cook's Tip
If necessary, keep the fish fillets warm by placing on a wire cooling rack covered with paper towels and place in a warm oven, leaving the door slightly ajar. Sprinkling the fish fillets lightly with salt as they drain on paper towels helps remove some of the oil.

Variations
Other whitefish fillets may be prepared in the same way. Choose fillets that are of even size so that they cook in the same length of time. Chopped onion may be substituted for the garlic, if desired.

SERVES 6-8

SEAFOOD TORTA

A very stylish version of a fish flan, this makes
a perfect accompaniment to an Italian aperitif or
serves as a light supper dish with salad.

Pastry

2 cups all-purpose flour, sifted
½ cup unsalted butter
Pinch salt
4 tbsps cold milk

Filling

4oz whitefish fillets (plaice, sole or cod)
8oz cooked shrimp
4oz flaked crab meat
½ cup white wine
½ cup water
Large pinch hot pepper flakes
Salt and pepper
2 tbsps butter
2 tbsps flour
1 clove garlic, crushed
2 egg yolks
½ cup heavy cream
Chopped fresh parsley

Step 5 Press a sheet of wax paper on the pastry and fill with beans, rice or baking beans to weight down.

1. To prepare the pastry, sift the flour into a bowl or onto a work surface. Cut the butter into small pieces and begin mixing them into the flour. Mix until the mixture resembles fine breadcrumbs – this may also be done in a food processor. Make a well in the flour, pour in the milk and add the pinch of salt. Mix with a fork, gradually incorporating the butter and flour mixture from the sides until all the ingredients are mixed. This may also be done in a food processor.

2. Form the dough into a ball and knead for about 1 minute. Leave the dough in the refrigerator for about 1 hour.

3. To prepare the filling, cook whitefish fillets in the water and wine with the red pepper flakes for about 10 minutes or until just firm to the touch. When the fish is cooked, remove it from the liquid and flake it into a bowl with the shrimp and the crab meat. Reserve the cooking liquid.

4. Melt the butter in a small saucepan and stir in the flour. Gradually strain on the cooking liquid from the fish, stirring constantly until smooth. Add garlic, place over high heat and bring to the boil. Lower the heat and allow to cook for 1 minute. Add to the fish in the bowl and set aside to cool.

5. On a well-floured surface, roll out the pastry and transfer it with a rolling pin to a tart pan with a removable base. Press the dough into the pan and cut off any excess. Prick the pastry base lightly with a fork and place a sheet of wax paper inside. Fill with rice, dried beans or baking beans and chill for 30 minutes. Bake the pastry shell blind for 15 minutes in a 375°F oven.

6. While the pastry is baking, combine the egg yolks, cream and parsley and stir into the fish filling. Adjust the seasoning with salt and pepper. When the pastry is ready, remove the paper and beans and pour in the filling.

7. Return the tart to the oven and bake for a further 25 minutes. Allow to cool slightly and then remove from the pan. Transfer to a serving dish and slice before serving.

Cook's Notes

Time
Filling takes about 15-20 minutes to prepare. Pastry takes about 20 minutes to prepare plus 1 hour refrigeration. Tart takes about 40 minutes to cook.

Variation
Substitute lobster for the whitefish for a special occasion or dinner party first course.

Freezing
Make the pastry in advance and wrap it very well. Label and freeze for up to 3 months. Defrost at room temperature before using. Also freeze uncooked in the flan dish.

SERVES 4

SARDINE AND TOMATO GRATINÉE

Fresh sardines are becoming more widely available and this
recipe makes the most of these delicious fish.

3 tbsps olive oil
2lbs large fresh sardines, descaled and cleaned
2 leeks, cleaned and sliced
½ cup dry white wine
8oz tomatoes, skinned and quartered
Salt and pepper
2 tbsps each chopped fresh basil and parsley
½ cup Parmesan cheese, grated
½ cup dry breadcrumbs

1. Heat the oil in a frying pan and fry the sardines, until they

are brown on both sides. It may be necessary to do this in
several batches, to prevent the fish from breaking up.

2. When all the sardines are cooked, set them aside and
cook the leeks gently in the sardine oil. When the leeks are
soft, pour in the wine and boil rapidly, until it is reduced by
about two thirds.

3. Add the tomatoes, seasoning and herbs to the leeks
and cook for about 1 minute. Pour the vegetables into an
ovenproof dish and lay the sardines on top.

4. Sprinkle the cheese and breadcrumbs evenly over the
sardines and bake in a preheated oven, 425°F, for about 5
minutes.

Step 1 Fry the
sardines a few at a
time, to prevent
them from
breaking up during
cooking.

Step 4 Sprinkle
the Parmesan
cheese and
breadcrumbs
evenly over the
sardines, before
baking them.

Cook's Notes

Time
Preparation takes about 20-25
minutes. Cooking takes about
15 minutes.

Variation
Try substituting herrings or
mackerel for the sardines.
They will take a little longer to fry.

Serving Ideas
Cut a few anchovy fillets in half
lengthways and arrange them
in a lattice on top of the gratinée, before
serving with hot garlic bread.

Freezing
Sardines can be frozen for up
to 2 months, but remember to
clean and descale them first.

SERVES 6

SHRIMP AND GINGER

Quick and easy to prepare, this dish is really delicious and
also very nutritious.

2 tbsps oil
1½lbs peeled shrimp
1-inch piece fresh root ginger, peeled and finely chopped
2 cloves of garlic, peeled and finely chopped
2-3 green onions, chopped
1 leek, white part only, cut into strips
¾ cup peas, shelled
3 cups bean sprouts
2 tbsps dark soy sauce
1 tsp sugar
Pinch salt

1. Heat the oil in a wok and stir-fry the shrimp for 2-3 minutes. Set the shrimp aside.

2. Reheat the oil and add the ginger and garlic. Stir quickly, then add the onions, leek and peas. Stir-fry for 2-3 minutes.

3. Add the bean sprouts and shrimp to the cooked vegetables. Stir in the soy sauce, sugar and salt and cook for 2 minutes. Serve immediately.

Step 2 Stir-fry the onions, leek and peas for 2-3 minutes.

Step 3 Cook all the ingredients together for 2 minutes before serving.

Cook's Notes

Time
Preparation takes about 10 minutes, and cooking takes about 7-9 minutes.

Preparation
The vegetables can be prepared in advance and kept in airtight plastic boxes in the refrigerator for up to 6 hours before needed.

Serving Ideas
Serve this on its own with rice or pasta, or as part of an authentic Chinese meal.

SERVES 4
TRUITE MEUNIÈRE AUX HERBES

The miller (meunier) caught trout fresh from the mill stream and his wife used the flour which was on hand to dredge them with, or so the story goes.

4 even-sized trout, cleaned and trimmed
Flour
Salt and pepper
½ cup butter
Juice of 1 lemon
2 tbsps chopped fresh herbs such as parsley, chervil, tarragon, thyme or marjoram
Lemon wedges to garnish

1. Trim the trout tails to make them more pointed. Rinse the trout well.

2. Dredge the trout with flour and shake off the excess. Season with salt and pepper. Heat half the butter in a very large sauté pan and, when foaming, place in the trout. It may be necessary to cook the trout in two batches to avoid overcrowding the pan.

3. Cook over fairly high heat on both sides to brown evenly. Depending on size, the trout should take 5-8 minutes per side to cook. The dorsal fin will pull out easily when the trout are cooked. Remove the trout to a serving dish and keep them warm.

4. Wipe out the pan and add the remaining butter. Cook over moderate heat until beginning to brown, then add the lemon juice and herbs. When the lemon juice is added, the butter will bubble up and sizzle. Pour immediately over the fish and serve with lemon wedges.

Step 1 Trim the trout tails with scissors to make them neater.

Step 2 Coat trout in flour, shaking off excess.

Step 3 Brown the trout on both sides. Dorsal fin will pull out easily when done.

Cook's Notes

Time
Preparation takes 15-20 minutes, cooking takes 5-8 minutes per side for the fish and about 5 minutes to brown the butter.

Preparation
If trout is coated in flour too soon before cooking it will become soggy.

Serving Ideas
Serve with new potatoes and peeled, cubed cucumber quickly sautéed in butter and chopped dill.

SERVES 4

BAKED STUFFED MACKEREL

Mackerel should be eaten the day it is caught, so this is a
recipe for people living near the sea.

¼ cup polyunsaturated margarine
1 small onion, finely chopped
1 tbsp medium oatmeal
⅓ cup fresh whole-wheat breadcrumbs
1½ tsps chopped fresh lemon thyme
1½ tsps chopped fresh parsley
Freshly ground sea salt and black pepper
2-3 tbsps hot water, if required
4 mackerel, cleaned and washed thoroughly

Step 1 Fry the chopped onion, until it is soft but not colored.

1. In a large frying pan, melt the margarine. Fry the chopped onion in the margarine until it is soft, but not colored.

2. Add the oatmeal, breadcrumbs, herbs and seasoning to the fried onion, and mix well to form a firm stuffing, adding a little hot water to bind, if necessary.

3. Fill the cavities of the fish with the stuffing and wrap each one separately in well-greased aluminum foil.

4. Place each fish parcel in a roasting pan, or on a cookie sheet, and cook in a preheated oven, 375°F, for half an hour.

Step 2 Add the oatmeal, breadcrumbs, herbs and seasoning to the fried onion, and mix well to form a firm stuffing, binding with a little of the hot water, if necessary.

Step 3 Fill the cavities of each fish with equal amounts of the onion and oatmeal stuffing. Push the stuffing well into the back of the fish to preserve its shape.

Cook's Notes

Time
Preparation takes about 15 minutes, and cooking takes about 30 minutes.

Variation
The stuffing in this recipe is also delicious with herrings, or whiting.

Serving Ideas
Serve this dish garnished with fresh watercress and new potatoes.

SERVES 4

COCONUT FRIED FISH WITH CHILIES

A real treat for lovers of spicy food.

Oil for frying
1lb sole or plaice fillets, skinned, boned and cut into
   1-inch strips
Seasoned flour
1 egg, beaten
¾ cup shredded coconut
1 tbsp vegetable oil
1 tsp grated fresh ginger
¼ tsp chili powder
1 red chili, seeded and finely chopped
1 tsp ground coriander
½ tsp ground nutmeg
1 clove garlic, crushed
2 tbsps tomato paste
2 tbsps tomato chutney
2 tbsps dark soy sauce
2 tbsps lemon juice
2 tbsps water
1 tsp brown sugar
Salt and pepper

Step 1 Toss the strips of fish in the flour and then dip them in the beaten egg. Roll them finally in the shredded coconut. Do not coat the fish too soon before frying.

Step 2 Fry the fish in the hot oil, a few pieces at a time, to prevent it from breaking up.

1. In a frying pan, heat about 2 inches of oil to 375°F. Toss the fish strips in the seasoned flour and then dip them into the beaten egg. Roll them in the shredded coconut and shake off the excess.

2. Fry the fish, a few pieces at a time, in the hot oil and drain them on paper towels. Keep warm.

3. Heat the 1 tbsp oil in a wok or frying pan and fry the ginger, red chili, spices and garlic, for about 2 minutes.

4. Add the remaining ingredients and simmer for about 3 minutes. Serve the fish, with the sauce handed round separately.

Cook's Notes

Time
Preparation takes about 30 minutes, and cooking takes about 30 minutes.

Cook's Tip
Great care should be taken when preparing fresh chilies. Always wash your hands thoroughly afterwards, and avoid getting any juice in your eyes or mouth. Rinse with copious amounts of clear water, if you do.

Variation
Substitute a firm fleshed fish like haddock, or monkfish, for the plaice.

Serving Ideas
Serve with plain boiled rice, a cucumber relish and plenty of salad.

Chapter IV

Regional Specialties

SERVES 4

TUNA BAKED IN PARCHMENT

This recipe uses a French technique called "en papillote".
Californians, quick to spot a healthful cooking
method, use it often with fish.

4 tuna steaks, about 8oz each in weight
1 red onion, thinly sliced
1 beefsteak tomato, cut in 4 slices
1 green pepper, seeded and cut in thin rings
8 large, uncooked peeled shrimp
2 tsps finely chopped fresh oregano
1 small green or red chili, seeded and finely chopped
4 tbsps dry white wine or lemon juice
Salt
Oil

Steps 1-4 Layer the ingredients on oiled parchment.

1. Lightly oil 4 oval pieces of baking parchment about 8x10".

2. Place a tuna steak on half of each piece of parchment and top with 2 slices of onion.

3. Place a slice of tomato on each fish and top with green pepper rings.

4. Place 2 shrimp on top and sprinkle over the oregano, salt and chili pepper.

5. Spoon the wine or lemon juice over each fish and fold the parchment over the fish.

6. Overlap the edges and pinch and fold to seal securely. Place the parcels on a baking sheet.

7. Bake for about 10-12 minutes in a pre-heated 400°F oven.

8. Unwrap each parcel at the table to serve.

Step 6 Overlap the edges of the parchment, but don't enclose fish too tightly.

Step 6 Use thumb and forefinger to pinch and fold the overlapped edge to seal.

Cook's Notes

Time
Preparation takes about 35 minutes and cooking takes about 10-12 minutes.

Preparation
The dish may be prepared up to 6 hours in advance and kept in the refrigerator. Remove about 30 minutes before cooking and allow fish to come to room temperature.

Variation
Other fish, such as swordfish or halibut, can be used in place of the tuna. Any thinly-sliced vegetable other than potato can be used.

SERVES 4

CRAWFISH PIE

This seafood, plentiful in southern Louisiana, is
used in many delicious ways. The boiling mixture adds
spice, and the browned flour a nutty taste and good color.

Pastry

2 cups all-purpose flour, sifted
Pinch salt
½-¾ cup butter or margarine
Cold water

1lb raw crawfish or shrimp
½ quantity spice mixture for Shellfish Boil (see recipe)

Filling

3 tbsps oil
3 tbsps flour
½ green pepper, seeded and finely diced
2 green onions, finely chopped
1 stick celery, finely chopped
1 cup light cream
Salt and pepper

Step 6 Roll the
pastry out thinly
and use a rolling
pin to transfer it to
the baking dish.

1. Sift the flour into a bowl with a pinch of salt and rub in the
butter or margarine until the mixture resembles fine
breadcrumbs. Add enough cold water to bring the mixture
together. Knead into a ball, wrap well and chill for about 30
minutes before use.

2. Combine the spice mixture with about 2½ cups water.
Bring to the boil and add the crawfish or shrimp. Cook for
about 5 minutes, stirring occasionally until the shellfish curl
up. Remove from the liquid and leave to drain.

3. Heat the oil in a small saucepan for the filling and add
the flour. Cook slowly, stirring constantly until the flour turns
a rich dark brown.

4. Add the remaining filling ingredients, stirring constantly
while adding the cream. Bring to the boil, reduce the heat
and cook for about 5 minutes. Add the crawfish or shrimp to
the sauce.

5. Divide the pastry into 4 and roll out each portion on a
lightly-floured surface to about ¼ inch thick.

6. Line individual flan or pie dishes with the pastry,
pushing it carefully onto the base and down the sides,
taking care not to stretch it. Trim off excess pastry and
reserve.

7. Place a sheet of wax paper or foil on the pastry and pour
on rice, pasta or baking beans to come halfway up the
sides. Bake the pastry blind for about 10 minutes in a preheated 400°F oven.

8. Remove the paper and beans and bake for an
additional 5 minutes to cook the base.

9. Spoon in the filling and roll out any trimmings to make a
lattice pattern on top. Bake a further 10 minutes to brown the
lattice and heat the filling. Cool slightly before serving.

Cook's Notes

 Time
Preparation takes about 30
minutes and cooking takes
about 10 minutes for the filling and 25
minutes to finish the dish.

Cook's Tip
Baking the pastry blind helps
it to crisp on the base and
brown evenly without overcooking the
filling.

 Serving Ideas
Serve as a light main course
with a salad, or make smaller
pies to serve as a first course.

SERVES 6

SEAFOOD GUMBO FILÉ

Either filé powder, made from sassafras leaves, or okra gives a Cajun gumbo its characteristic texture. Gumbos are good without filé, too.

1lb cooked, unpeeled shrimp
Half quantity spice mixture (see Shellfish Boil)
5 cups water
4 tbsps butter or margarine
1 onion, peeled and sliced
1 green pepper, seeded and sliced
2 cloves garlic, finely chopped
3 tbsps flour
½ tsp thyme
1 bay leaf
2 tbsps chopped parsley
Dash Worcester sauce
12 oysters, shelled
8oz tomatoes, peeled and chopped
2 tbsps filé powder (optional)
Salt and pepper
Cooked rice

1. Peel the shrimp and reserve the shells. Mix shells with the spice mixture and water and bring to the boil in a large stock pot. Reduce the heat and allow to simmer for about 20 minutes.

2. Melt the butter or margarine and, when foaming, add the onion, green pepper, garlic and flour. Cook slowly, stirring constantly until the flour is a pale golden brown. Gradually strain on the stock, discarding the shells and spice mixture. Add the thyme and bay leaf and stir well. Bring to the boil and then simmer until thick.

Step 1 Peel the shrimp adding the heads, tail shell, legs and roe, if present, to the spice mixture in a large stock pot.

Step 3 Loosen the oysters from their shells and add to the hot gumbo. If desired, strain the oyster liquid through a very fine mesh strainer.

3. Add the parsley and the Worcester sauce to taste. Add the oysters, peeled shrimp and tomatoes and heat through gently to cook the oysters.

4. Stir in the filé powder and leave to stand to thicken. Adjust the seasoning and serve over rice.

Cook's Notes

Time
Preparation takes about 25-30 minutes and cooking takes about 20-25 minutes.

Variation
If they are available, use raw, unpeeled shrimp and cook with the water and the spice mixture until they turn pink and curl up. Drain them, reserving the liquid. Peel and return the shells to the stock. Re-boil the stock and allow to simmer for about 15 minutes.

Cook's Tip
If filé powder is not available, use equal portions of butter or margarine and flour mixed together to a paste. Add a bit of the paste at a time to the gumbo, and boil in between additions until the desired thickness is reached.

CALIFORNIAN SHRIMP AND SCALLOP STIR-FRY

Stir-frying came to California with Chinese settlers who worked on the railroads. It's the perfect way to cook seafood.

3 tbsps oil
4 tbsps pine nuts
1lb uncooked shrimp
1lb shelled scallops, quartered if large
2 tsps grated fresh ginger
1 small red or green chili, seeded and finely chopped
2 cloves garlic, finely chopped
1 large red pepper, seeded and cut into 1″ diagonal
    pieces
8oz fresh spinach, stalks removed and leaves well
    washed and shredded
4 green onions, cut in ½″ diagonal pieces
4 tbsps fish or chicken stock
4 tbsps light soy sauce
4 tbsps rice wine or dry sherry
1 tbsp cornstarch

1. Heat oil in a wok and add the pine nuts. Cook over low heat, stirring continuously until lightly browned. Remove with a draining spoon and drain on paper towels.

2. Add the shrimp and scallops to the oil remaining in the wok and stir over moderate heat until shellfish is beginning to look opaque and firm and the shrimp look pink.

3. Add the ginger, chili, garlic and red pepper and cook a few minutes over moderately high heat.

4. Add the spinach and onion, and stir-fry briefly. Mix the remaining ingredients together and pour over the ingredients in the wok.

5. Turn up the heat to bring the liquid quickly to the boil, stirring ingredients constantly. Once the liquid thickens and clears, stir in the pine nuts and serve immediately.

Step 1 Cook pine nuts in oil until they are light brown.

Step 2 Cook shellfish until shrimp begin to turn pink and scallops lose their transparency.

Step 5 When all ingredients are added, cook briskly to thicken the sauce.

Cook's Notes

Time
Preparation takes about 35 minutes, cooking takes about 8-10 minutes.

Preparation
Because cooking time is so short, be sure to prepare all ingredients and have them ready before beginning to stir-fry.

Economy
Eliminate scallops and cut the quantity of shrimp in half. Make up the difference with a firm whitefish cut into 1″ pieces.

SERVES 4-6

SHELLFISH BOIL

This is the Cajun way to cook seafood.
Drained seafood is piled onto newspaper-covered
tables for everyone to dig in.

3 quarts water
1 lemon, quartered
1 onion, cut in half but not peeled
1 celery stick, cut in 3 pieces
2 cloves garlic, left whole
Pinch salt
4 bay leaves, finely crumbled
4 dried red chili peppers, crumbled
1 tbsp each whole cloves, whole allspice, coriander seed
   and mustard seed
1 tbsp dill weed, fresh or dry
2 tsps celery seed
1lb raw, unpeeled shrimp
2lbs mussels, well scrubbed

Step 3 Remove the seaweed beards and any barnacles from the mussel shells.

Step 2 Add the shrimp to the boiling liquid and cook them until pink and curled.

1. Place the water, lemon, onion, celery, garlic, salt, bay leaves and spices together in a large pot and cover. Bring to the boil, reduce the heat and cook slowly for 20 minutes.

2. Add the shrimp in two batches and cook until pink and curled. Remove with a draining spoon.

3. Remove the seaweed beards from the mussels, and discard any that do not close when tapped.

4. Add mussels to the pot and cook, stirring frequently, for about 5 minutes or until shells have opened. Discard any that do not open.

5. Spoon shrimp and mussels into serving bowls and serve immediately.

Cook's Notes

Time
Preparation takes about 30 minutes, cooking takes about 20 minutes to boil the stock and about 5 minutes for each batch of shrimp and mussels.

Serving Ideas
Serve as an appetizer, or double the quantity for a main course.

Variation
Usually crawfish are cooked in this way. Crabs are also used.

SERVES 4

BLACKENED FISH

Cajun cooks all have their own special recipes for the spice mixture, but all agree that the food should have a *very* brown crust when properly blackened.

4 fish steaks or fillets, about 8oz each
1 cup unsalted butter
1 tbsps parika
1 tsp garlic powder
1 tsp cayenne powder
½ tsp ground white pepper
1 tsp finely ground black pepper
2 tsps salt
1 tsp dried thyme

5. Turn the fish over when the underside is very brown and repeat with the remaining side. Add more butter as necessary during cooking.

6. When the top side of the fish is very dark brown, repeat with the remaining fish fillets, keeping them warm while cooking the rest.

7. Serve the fish immediately with the cups of butter for dipping.

Step 2 Use a pastry brush to coat the fish well on both sides with the melted butter. Alternatively spoon the butter over or dip the fish in the butter.

Step 3 Mix the seasoning ingredients together well and press firmly onto both sides of the fish to coat.

Step 5 Cook the underside and topside of the fish until very dark brown.

1. Melt the butter and pour about half into each of four custard cups and set aside.

2. Brush each fish steak liberally with the remaining butter on both sides.

3. Mix together the spices and thyme and sprinkle generously on each side of the steaks, patting it on by hand.

4. Heat a large frying pan and add about 1 tbsp butter per fish steak. When the butter is hot, add the fish, skin side down first.

Cook's Notes

Time
Preparation takes about 20 minutes and cooking takes about 2 minutes per side for each fillet.

Variation
Red fish or pompano is the usual choice. If these fish are not available, substitute other varieties of fish fillets or steaks that are approximately ¾ inch thick.

Preparation
The fish must be very dark brown on the top and the bottom before serving. Leave at least 2 minutes before attempting to turn the fish over.

SERVES 4

BOILED MAINE LOBSTER

With today's lobster prices, it's hard to
imagine that American colonists considered
this delectable seafood humble and ordinary.

4 1lb lobsters
Water
Salt or seaweed
1 cup melted butter
Lemon wedges
Parsley sprigs

Step 6 Separate body from tail by arching the lobster backwards. Break off the flipper and push the tail meat out with a fork.

Step 5 Once the claws are removed from the lobster by twisting off, crack each claw with a nutcracker, hammer or special lobster cracking tool.

Step 7 Remove the back from the body and discard the stomach sac and lungs. Retain the tomalley or liver to eat, if desired, and crack open the body to extract any remaining meat.

1. Fill a large stock pot full of water and add salt or a piece of seaweed. Bring the water to the boil and then turn off the heat.

2. Place the live lobsters into the pot, keeping your hand well away from the claws. Lower them in claws first.

3. Bring the water slowly back to the boil and cook the

lobsters for about 15 minutes, or until they turn bright red.

4. Remove them from the water and drain briefly on paper towels. Place on a plate and garnish the plate with lemon wedges and parsley sprigs. Serve with individual dishes of melted butter for dipping.

Cook's Notes

Time
Allow about 20 minutes for the water to boil, and 15 minutes for cooking the lobster.

Preparation
This method of cooking puts the lobster gently to sleep and makes the lobster flesh much more tender. Claws can be partially cracked before serving, if desired.

Cook's Tip
Lobster may be cooked in this way for a variety of recipes that are based on pre-cooked lobster.

SERVES 4

BOSTON SCROD

Scrod, or baby codfish, provides the perfect
base for a crunchy, slightly spicy topping.
Boston is justly famous for it.

4 even-sized cod fillets
Salt and pepper
⅓ cup butter, melted
¾ cup dry breadcrumbs
1 tsp dry mustard
1 tsp onion salt
Dash Worcester sauce and tabasco
2 tbsps lemon juice
1 tbsp finely chopped parsley

Step 3 Press the crumbs gently to pack them into place using a spoon or your hand.

Step 1 Season the fish lightly with salt and pepper and brush with some of the melted butter. Broil to pre-cook but do not brown.

1. Season the fish fillets with salt and pepper and place them on a broiler tray. Brush with butter and broil for about 5 minutes.

2. Combine remaining butter with breadcrumbs, mustard, onion salt, Worcester sauce, tabasco, lemon juice and parsley.

3. Spoon the mixture carefully on top of each fish fillet, covering it completely. Press down lightly to pack the crumbs into place. Broil for a further 5-7 minutes, or until the top is lightly browned and the fish flakes.

Cook's Notes

Time
Preparation takes about 15 minutes and cooking takes about 12 minutes.

Preparation
If desired, the fish may also be baked in the oven Cover the fish with foil for first 5 minutes of baking time, uncover and top with the breadcrumb mixture. Bake for a further 10-12 minutes at 350°F.

Variation
The breadcrumb topping may be used on other fish such as haddock, halibut or sole.

SERVES 4

SNAPPER WITH FENNEL AND ORANGE SALAD

Red snapper brings Florida to mind. Combined with oranges, it makes a lovely summer meal.

Oil
4 even-sized red snapper, cleaned, heads and tails on
2 heads fennel
2 oranges
Juice of 1 lemon
3 tbsps light salad oil
Pinch sugar, salt and black pepper

1. Brush both sides of the fish with oil and cut three slits in the sides of each. Sprinkle with a little of the lemon juice, reserving the rest.

2. Slice the fennel in half and remove the cores. Slice thinly. Also slice the green tops and chop the feathery herb to use in the dressing.

3. Peel the oranges, removing all the white pith.

4. Cut the oranges into segments. Peel and segment over

a bowl to catch the juice.

5. Add lemon juice to any orange juice collected in the bowl. Add the oil, salt, pepper and a pinch of sugar, if necessary. Mix well and add the fennel, green herb tops and orange segments, stirring carefully. Broil the fish 3-5 minutes per side, depending on thickness. Serve the fish with the heads and tails on, accompanied by the salad.

Step 2 Slice the fennel in half and remove the cores.

Step 4 Peel and segment the oranges over a bowl to catch the juice.

Cook's Notes

Time
Preparation takes about 30 minutes and cooking takes about 6-10 minutes.

Variation
Other fish may be used in the recipe if snapper is not available. Substitute red mullet or any of the exotic fish from the Seychelles Islands or Hawaii.

Cook's Tip
When broiling whole fish, making several cuts on the side of each fish will help to cook it quickly and evenly throughout.

SERVES 6-8

CIOPPINO

California's famous and delicious fish
stew is Italian in heritage; but a close
relative of French Bouillabaisse, too.

1lb spinach, well washed
1 tbsp each chopped fresh basil, thyme, rosemary and
    sage
2 tbsps chopped fresh marjoram
4 tbsps chopped parsley
1 large red pepper, seeded and finely chopped
2 cloves garlic, crushed
24 large fresh clams or 48 mussels, well scrubbed
1 large crab, cracked
1lb monkfish or rock salmon (huss)
12 large shrimp, cooked and unpeeled
1lb canned plum tomatoes and juice
2 tbsps tomato paste
4 tbsps olive oil
Pinch salt and pepper
½-1 cup dry white wine
Water

1. Chop the spinach leaves roughly after removing any
tough stems.

2. Combine the spinach with the herbs, chopped red
pepper and garlic, and set aside.

3. Discard any clams or mussels with broken shells or
ones that do not close when tapped. Place the shellfish in
the bottom of a large pot and sprinkle over a layer of the
spinach mixture.

4. Prepare the crab as for Crab Louis, leaving the shells on
the claws after cracking them slightly. Place the crab on top
of the spinach and then add another spinach layer.

5. Add the fish and a spinach layer, followed by the shrimp
and any remaining spinach.

6. Mix the tomatoes, tomato paste, oil, wine and seasonings and pour over the seafood and spinach.

7. Cover the pot and simmer the mixture for about 40
minutes. If more liquid is necessary, add water. Spoon into
soup bowls, dividing the fish and shell fish evenly.

Step 3 Place well
scrubbed clams
or mussels in the
bottom of a large
pot, sprinkling
over spinach
mixture.

Step 6 Pour the
tomato paste and
wine mixture over
the layered
seafood and
spinach

Cook's Notes

Time
Preparation takes abut 40
minutes and cooking takes
about 40 minutes.

Preparation
Soup must be eaten
immediately after cooking. It
does not keep or reheat well.

Variation
The choice of seafood or fish
may be changed to suit your
own taste and budget. For special
occasions, add lobster.

Chapter V

ENTERTAINING

SWORDFISH WITH GRAPEFRUIT TEQUILA SALSA

Rich and dense in texture, swordfish takes very well to a tart grapefruit accompaniment with a dash of tequila.

4-6 ruby or pink grapefruit (depending on size)
1 lime
Half a green chili, seeded and finely sliced
1 green onion, finely chopped
2 tbsps chopped fresh coriander
1 tbsps sugar
3 tbsps tequila
4-8 swordfish steaks (depending on size)
Juice of 1 lime
2 tbsps oil
Black pepper to taste
Coriander sprigs for garnish

1. Remove the zest from the grapefruit and lime with a zester and set it aside.

2. Remove all the pith from the grapefruit and segment them. Squeeze the lime for juice. Mix the grapefruit and citrus zests with the chili, onion, coriander, sugar, tequila and lime juice and set aside.

3. Mix remaining lime juice, oil and pepper together and brush both sides of the fish. Place under a pre-heated broiler and cook for about 4 minutes each side depending on distance from the heat source.

4. To serve, place a coriander sprig on each fish steak and serve with the grapefruit salsa.

Step 1 Remove the zest from the grapefruit with a zester.

Step 2 use a serrated fruit knife to remove all the pith from the grapefruit.

Cook's Notes

Time
Preparation takes about 35 minutes and cooking takes about 4-6 minutes.

Variation
If desired, substitute white rum for the tequila in the salsa or omit it altogether. The amount of sugar needed will vary depending on the sweetness of the grapefruit.

Cook's Tip
For extra flavor, the swordfish steaks may be marinated in a lime juice and oil mixture for up to 1 hour.

SERVES 4

SEAFOOD PAN ROAST

This mixture of oysters and crab is a descendant
of French gratin recipes. It's quick to make,
and other seafood may be added.

24 small oysters on the half shell
1 cup fish stock
1 cup light cream
⅓ cup butter or margarine
6 tbsps flour
1 bunch green onions, chopped
2oz parsley, chopped
2 tbsps Worcester sauce
½ tsp tabasco
Pinch salt
1 large or 2 small cooked crabs
4 slices bread, crusts trimmed and made into crumbs

Step 3 Turn the crabs over and push out the body with your thumbs.

1. Remove the oysters from their shells with a small, sharp knife. Place the oysters in a saucepan and strain over any oyster liquid. Add the fish stock and cook gently until the oysters curl around the edges. Remove the oysters, keep them warm and strain the liquid into a clean pan.

2. Add the cream to the oyster liquid and bring to the boil. Allow to boil rapidly for about 5 minutes.

3. Remove crab claws and legs. Turn the crabs over and push out the body with your thumbs.

4. Remove the stomach sac and lungs (dead man's fingers) and discard.

5. Cut the body in four sections with a large, sharp knife and pick out the meat with a skewer.

6. Crack claws and legs to extract the meat. Leave the small legs whole for garnish, if desired.

7. Scrape out the brown meat from inside the shell and combine it with the breadcrumbs and white meat from the body and claws.

8. Melt the butter or margarine in a medium-size saucepan and stir in the flour. Cook gently for 5 minutes. Add the onions and parsley and cook a further 5 minutes. Pour over the cream and fish stock mixture, stirring constantly. Add the Worcester sauce, tabasco and salt, and cook about 15-20 minutes over low heat, stirring occasionally. Fold in the crab meat and breadcrumb mixture.

9. Place the oysters in the bottom of a buttered casserole or in individual dishes and spoon the crab meat mixture on top. Broil to brown, if desired, and serve immediately.

Cook's Notes

Time
Preparation takes about 40 minutes and cooking takes about 30 minutes.

Buying Guide
If fresh oysters on the half shell and freshly cooked crabs are not available, substitute canned oysters and use their liquid for part of the fish stock measurement. Canned oysters will not need as long to cook. Canned or frozen crab meat may be used in place of the fresh crabs, substituting about 8oz for the fresh crab meat.

Serving Ideas
If serving as a first course, this recipe will serve 6. Add French bread and a salad for a light main course.

SERVES 6

SZECHUAN FISH

The piquant spiciness of Szechuan pepper is quite different from that of black or white pepper. Beware, though, too much can numb the mouth temporarily!

1lb whitefish fillets
Pinch salt and pepper
1 egg
5 tbsps flour
6 tbsps white wine
Oil for frying
2oz cooked ham, cut in small dice
1 inch piece fresh ginger, finely diced
½-1 red or green chili pepper, cored, seeded and finely diced
6 water chestnuts, finely diced
4 green onions, finely chopped
3 tbsps light soy sauce
1 tsp cider vinegar or rice wine vinegar
½ tsp ground Szechuan pepper (optional)
1 cup light stock
1 tbsp cornstarch dissolved with 2 tbsps water
2 tsps sugar

1. To prepare the garnish, choose unblemished chili peppers with the stems on. Using a small, sharp knife, cut the peppers in strips, starting from the pointed end.

2. Cut down to within ½ inch of the stem end. Rinse out the seeds under cold running water and place the peppers in iced water.

3. Leave the peppers to soak for at least 4 hours or overnight until they open up like flowers.

4. Cut the fish fillets into 2 inch pieces and season with salt and pepper. Beat the egg well and add flour and wine to make a batter. Dredge the fish lightly with flour and then dip into the batter. Mix the fish well.

5. Heat a wok and when hot, add enough oil to deep-fry the fish. When the oil is hot, fry a few pieces of fish at a time, until golden brown. Drain and proceed until all the fish is cooked.

6. Remove all but 1 tbsp of oil from the wok and add the ham, ginger, diced chili pepper, water chestnuts and green onions. Cook for about 1 minute and add the soy sauce and vinegar. If using Szechuan pepper, add at this point. Stir well and cook for a further 1 minute. Remove the vegetables from the pan and set them aside.

7. Add the stock to the wok and bring to the boil. When boiling, add 1 spoonful of the hot stock to the cornstarch mixture. Add the mixture back to the stock and reboil, stirring constantly until thickened.

8. Stir in the sugar and return the fish and vegetables to the sauce. Heat through for 30 seconds and serve at once.

Step 1 Cut the tip of each chili pepper into strips.

Step 3 Allow to soak 4 hours or overnight to open up.

Cook's Notes

Time
Preparation takes about 30 minutes. Chili pepper garnish takes at least 4 hours to soak. Cooking takes about 10 minutes.

Serving Ideas
Serve with plain or fried rice. Do not eat the chili pepper garnish.

Buying Guide
Szechuan peppercorns are available in Chinese supermarkets or delicatessens. If not available, substitute extra chili pepper.

SERVES 6

KUNG PAO SHRIMP WITH CASHEW NUTS

It is said that Kung Pao invented this dish,
but to this day no one knows who he was!

½ tsp chopped fresh ginger
1 tsp chopped garlic
1½ tbsps cornstarch
¼ tsp bicarbonate of soda
Salt and pepper
¼ tsp sugar
1lb uncooked shrimp
4 tbsps oil
1 small onion, cut into dice
1 large or 2 small zucchini, cut into ½ inch cubes
1 small red pepper, cut into ½ inch cubes
½ cup cashew nuts

Sauce

¾ cup chicken stock
1 tbsp cornstarch
2 tsps chili sauce
2 tsps bean paste (optional)
2 tsps sesame oil
1 tbsp dry sherry or rice wine

1. Mix together the ginger, garlic, 1½ tbsps cornstarch, bicarbonate of soda, salt, pepper and sugar.

2. If the shrimp are unpeeled, remove the peels and the dark vein running along the rounded side. If large, cut in half, Place in the dry ingredients and leave to stand for 20 minutes.

3. Heat the oil in a wok and when hot add the shrimp. Cook, stirring over high heat for about 20 seconds, or just until the shrimp change color. Transfer to a plate.

4. Add the onion to the same oil in the wok and cook for about 1 minute. Add the zucchini and red pepper and cook about 30 seconds.

5. Mix the sauce ingredients together and add to the wok. Cook, stirring constantly, until the sauce is slightly thickened. Add the shrimp and the cashew nuts and heat through completely.

Step 4 To dice the zucchini quickly, top and tail and cut into ½ inch strips.

Step 4 Cut the strips across with a large sharp knife into ½ inch pieces.

Cook's Notes

Time
Preparation takes about 20 minutes, cooking takes about 3 minutes.

Variation
If using cooked shrimp, add with the vegetables. Vary amount of chili sauce to suit your taste.

Serving Ideas
Serve with plain or fried rice.

SERVES 4

SWORDFISH FLORENTINE

Swordfish, with its dense texture, is a
perfect and healthful substitute for meat.
Here it has a distinctly Mediterranean flavor.

4 swordfish steaks about 6-8oz each in weight
Salt, pepper and lemon juice
Olive oil
2lbs fresh spinach, stems removed and leaves well
washed

Aioli Sauce

2 egg yolks
1-2 cloves garlic
Salt, pepper and dry mustard
Pinch cayenne pepper
1 cup olive oil
Lemon juice or white wine vinegar

1. Sprinkle fish with pepper, lemon juice and olive oil. Place under a pre-heated broiler and cook for about 3-4 minutes per side. Fish may also be cooked on an outdoor barbeque grill.

2. Meanwhile, use a sharp knife to shred the spinach finely. Place in a large saucepan and add a pinch of salt. Cover and cook over moderate heat with only the water that clings to the leaves after washing. Cook about 2 minutes, or until leaves are just slightly wilted. Set aside.

3. Place egg yolks in a food processor, blender or cup of a hand blender. Add the garlic, crushed, if using a hand blender. Process several times to mix eggs and purée garlic. Add salt, pepper, mustard and cayenne pepper. With the machine running, pour oil through the funnel in a thin, steady stream. Follow manufacturer's directions if using a hand blender.

4. When the sauce becomes very thick, add some lemon juice or vinegar in small quantities.

5. To serve, place a bed of spinach on a plate and top with the swordfish. Spoon some of the aioli sauce on top of the fish and serve the rest separately.

Step 3 Pour the oil for the sauce onto the egg yolks in a thin, steady stream.

Cook's Notes

Time
Preparation takes about 25 minutes and cooking takes about 6-8 minutes.

Variation
Fresh tuna may be used in place of the swordfish.

Preparation
The aioli or garlic mayonnaise may be prepared in advance and will keep for 5-7 days in the refrigerator. It is also delicious served with poached shellfish, chicken or vegetables. If too thick, thin the sauce with hot water.

SERVES 4

SPICED SALMON STEAKS

A blend of spices and sugar makes this easy-to-prepare
salmon dish very out of the ordinary.

½ cup of light brown sugar
1 tbsp ground allspice
1 tbsp mustard powder
1 tbsps grated fresh ginger
4 salmon steaks, 1 inch thick
1 cucumber
1 bunch green onions
2 tbsps butter
1 tbsp lemon juice
2 tsps chooped fresh dill weed
1 tbsp chopped fresh parsley
Salt and pepper

1. Mix the sugar and spices together and rub the mixture into the surface of both sides of the salmon steaks. Allow the salmon steaks to stand for at least 1 hour in the refrigerator.

2. Meanwhile prepare the vegetables. Peel the cucumber and cut into quarters lengthways. Remove the seeds and cut each quarter into 1 inch pieces.

3. Trim the roots from the green onions and cut down some, but not all, of the green part.

4. Put the cucumber and green onions into a saucepan, along with the butter, lemon juice, dill, parsley and seasoning. Cook over a moderate heat for about 10 minutes, or until the cucumber is tender and turning translucent.

5. Put the salmon steaks under a preheated moderate broiler and cook for about 5-6 minutes on each side.

6. Serve with the cucumber and green onion accompaniment.

Step 1 Rub the sugar and spice mixture into both surfaces of each salmon steak.

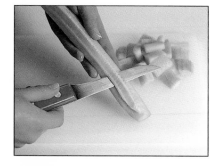

Step 2 Cut the peeled cucumber into quarters lengthways. Remove the seeds and cut each strip into 1-inch lengths.

Step 4 Cook the cucumber and onion with the herbs, flavorings, and butter until the cucumber is beginning to soften and become translucent.

Cook's Notes

Time
Preparation takes about 15 minutes, plus standing time of 1 hour, and cooking takes 12-15 minutes.

Preparation
The salmon steaks are ideal for cooking on an outdoor barbeque.

Variation
Substitute cod or haddock steaks for the salmon.

SERVES 4

MUSSELS À LA GRECQUE

Fresh mussels are a real treat during the autumn and winter
and the sauce in this recipe is a
reminder of warmer days!

4 cups mussels
1 onion, chopped
½ cup white wine
Lemon juice
2 tbsps olive oil
1 clove garlic, crushed
1 shallot or 2 green onions, chopped
1½lbs fresh tomatoes, chopped
1 tsp fennel seeds
1 tsp coriander seeds
1 tsp crushed oregano
1 bay leaf
1 tbsp chopped fresh basil
Pinch cayenne pepper
Salt and pepper
Black olives, to garnish

Step 5 Boil the tomato mixture rapidly, until the sauce has reduced and is thick and pulpy.

Step 2 Cook the mussels quickly, until all the shells are open, about 8 minutes. Discard any with shells that stay shut after this time.

1. Scrub the mussels and discard any with broken shells, or which do not shut when tapped with a knife.

2. Put them into a large saucepan with the onion, wine and lemon juice. Cover and cook quickly until the mussels open, discarding any that do not.

3. Remove the mussels from their shells and leave to cool. Reserve the cooking liquid.

4. Heat the olive oil in saucepan and add the garlic and the shallot, or green onions. Cook gently, until golden brown.

5. Stir in the tomatoes, spices and herbs. Season to taste and blend in the reserved liquor from the mussels. Bring this mixture to the boil and allow to boil rapidly, until the tomatoes are soft and the liquid is reduced by half. Remove the bay leaf.

6. Allow the sauce to cool, then stir in the mussels. Chill well and serve garnished with black olives.

Cook's Notes

Time
Preparation takes about 20 minutes, including cleaning the mussels. Cooking will take about 20 minutes.

Serving Ideas
Serve with a green salad and French bread.

Preparation
The shells of fresh mussels must be tightly closed and intact. Any that are cracked or do not shut tight when tapped with a knife should be thrown away. Any mussels that stay shut after being cooked, should also be discarded.

Cook's Tip
To keep mussels fresh overnight, wrap them in a thick layer of damp newspaper. Put this inside a polythene bag and store them in the bottom of a refrigerator. DO NOT KEEP FRESH SHELLFISH FOR ANY LONGER THAN OVERNIGHT.

SERVES 4

MONKFISH AND PEPPER KEBABS WITH BEARNAISE BUTTER SAUCE

Monkfish is a firm, succulent whitefish, ideal for kebabs.

8 strips bacon, boned and rind removed
2 pieces lemon grass
2lbs monkfish, cut into 2-inch pieces
1 green pepper, seeded and cut into 2-inch pieces
1 red pepper, seeded and cut into 2-inch pieces
12 button mushrooms, washed and trimmed
8 bay leaves
Oil for brushing
½ cup dry white wine
4 tbsps tarragon vinegar
2 shallots, finely chopped
1 tbsp chopped fresh tarragon
1 tbsp chopped fresh chervil or parsley
1 cup butter, melted
Salt and pepper

1. Cut the bacon in half lengthways and then in half across. Peel the lemon grass and use only the core. Cut this into small shreds.

2. Place a piece of fish on each strip of bacon and top with a shred of lemon grass. Roll up the bacon around the fish. Thread each fish and bacon roll onto kebab skewers, alternating with the pepper, mushrooms and bay leaves. Brush well with oil.

3. Cook under a moderate broiler for 15 minutes, turning frequently and brushing with more oil, if necessary, until the fish is cooked.

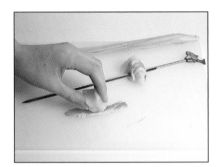

Step 2 Place a piece of fish onto a strip of bacon and top with a shred of lemon grass. Roll and thred onto kebab skewers.

Step 5 Stir the herbs into the reduced wine mixture. Lower the heat and beat in the butter, bit by bit, until the sauce is thick and creamy.

4. Heat together the wine, vinegar and shallots in a small saucepan until they are boiling. Cook rapidly until reduced by half.

5. Stir in the herbs and lower the heat. Beat in the butter, a little at a time, until the sauce is the thickness of an Hollandaise. Season to taste and serve with the kebabs.

Cook's Notes

Time
Preparation takes about 30 minutes, and cooking takes about 25 minutes.

Preparation
These kebabs are ideal for cooking over a barbecue.

Serving Ideas
Serve with a large mixed salad and rice, or pasta.

SERVES 4

RED MULLET WITH HERB AND MUSHROOM SAUCE

This is a Mediterranean fish with a slight taste of shrimp.
It is often cooked with the liver left in − a delicacy.

1lb small mushrooms, left whole
1 clove garlic, finely chopped
3 tbsps olive oil
Juice of 1 lemon
1 tbsp finely chopped parsley
2 tsps finely chopped basil
1 tsp finely chopped marjoram or sage
4 tbsps dry white wine mixed with ½ tsp cornstarch
Few drops anchovy paste
4 red mullet, each weighing about 8oz
2 tsps white breadcrumbs
2 tsps freshly grated Parmesan cheese

1. Combine the mushrooms, garlic and olive oil in a small frying pan. Cook over moderate heat for about 1 minute, until the garlic and mushrooms are slightly softened. Add all the herbs, lemon juice and white wine and cornstarch mixture. Bring to the boil and cook until thickened. Add anchovy paste to taste. Set aside while preparing the fish.

2. To clean the fish, cut along the stomach from the gills to the vent, the small hole near the tail. Clean out the cavity of the fish, leaving the liver, if desired.

3. To remove the gills, lift the flap and snip them out with a sharp pair of scissors. Rinse the fish well and pat dry.

4. Place the fish head to tail in a shallow ovenproof dish that can be used for serving. The fish should fit snugly into the dish.

5. Pour the prepared sauce over the fish and sprinkle with the breadcrumbs and Parmesan cheese.

6. Cover the dish loosely with foil and cook in the pre-heated oven at 375°F, for about 20 minutes. Uncover for the last 5 minutes, if desired, and raise the oven temperature slightly. This will lightly brown the fish.

Step 3 Lift the flap over the gills and use kitchen scissors to snip the gills away.

Step 4 Place the fish head to tail in a shallow baking dish just large enough to accommodate them.

Cook's Notes

 Time
Preparation takes about 30 minutes, cooking takes about 5 minutes for the sauce and 20 minutes for the fish.

 Preparation
If the fish need to be scaled, use the blunt edge of a knife and scrape from the tail to the head. Rinse well and remove any loose scales.

Variations
Use other fish such as bream or sardines.

SERVES 4

GRILLED FISH

Grilling fish with herbs and lemon is one of the most delightful ways of preparing it, and is particularly common in the Greek Islands.

2 large bream or other whole fish
Fresh thyme and oregano
Olive oil
Lemon juice
Salt and pepper
Lemon wedges
Vine leaves

1. Preheat a broiler. Gut the fish and rinse it well. Pat dry and sprinkle the cavity with salt, pepper and lemon juice. Place sprigs of herbs inside.

2. Make 3 diagonal cuts on the sides of the fish with a sharp knife. Place the fish on the broiler rack and sprinkle with olive oil and lemon juice.

3. Cook on both sides until golden brown and crisp. This should take about 8-10 minutes per side, depending on the thickness of the fish.

To make perfect lemon wedges, first cut the ends off the lemons, then cut in 4 or 8 wedges and remove the membrane and seeds.

Step 1 Open the cavity of the fish and sprinkle with salt, pepper and lemon juice.

Step 2 Use a sharp knife to make diagonal cuts on both sides of each fish.

4. If using vine leaves preserved in brine, rinse them well. If using fresh vine leaves, pour over boiling water and leave to stand for about 10 minutes to soften slightly. Drain and allow to cool. Line a large serving platter with the vine leaves and when the fish is cooked place it on top of the leaves. Serve surrounded with lemon wedges.

Cook's Notes

Time
Preparation takes about 20 minutes, cooking takes about 16-20 minutes, depending upon the size of the fish.

Cook's Tip
When broiling large whole fish, slit the skin on both sides to help the fish cook evenly.

Variation
The fish may be wrapped in vine leaves before broiling. This keeps the fish moist and adds extra flavor. Other fish suitable for cooking by this method are red mullet, trout, sea bass, gray mullet, sardines, herring or mackerel.

Preparation
If desired, the fish may be cooked on an outdoor barbecue grill. Wait until the coals have white ash on the top and be sure to oil the racks before placing on the fish, or use a special wire cage for cooking fish.

SERVES 4

RIVERSIDE TROUT

Brook trout is so delicious that simple preparation is all that's necessary. Crisp cornmeal, bacon and pine nuts complement the fresh flavor.

⅓-½ cup vegetable oil
4 tbsps pine nuts
8 strips bacon, diced
1 cup yellow cornmeal
Pinch salt and white pepper
4 trout weighing about 8oz each, cleaned
Juice of 1 lime
Fresh sage or coriander

1. Heat 6 tbsps of the oil in a large frying pan. Add the pine nuts and cook over moderate heat, stirring constantly. When a pale golden brown, remove them with a draining spoon to paper towels.

2. Add the diced bacon to the oil and cook until crisp, stirring constantly. Drain with the pine nuts.

3. Mix the cornmeal, salt and pepper, and dredge the fish well, patting on the cornmeal. Shake off any excess.

4. If necessary, add more oil to the pan – it should come about halfway up the sides of the fish. Re-heat over moderately high heat.

5. When hot, add the fish two at a time and fry until golden brown, about 4-5 minutes. Turn over and reduce the heat slightly if necessary and cook a further 4-5 minutes. Drain and repeat with the remaining fish.

6. Drain almost all the oil from the pan and re-heat the bacon and the nuts very briefly. Add the lime juice and cook a few seconds. Spoon the bacon and pine nut mixture over the fish and garnish with coriander or sage.

Step 3 Dredge the fish with the cornmeal mixture, shaking off any excess.

Step 5 Place the fish two at a time in hot oil and fry until golden brown on one side, then turn.

Step 6 Spoon the bacon, pine nut and lime juice mixture over the fish.

Cook's Notes

Time
Preparation takes about 25 minutes and cooking takes about 15-20 minutes.

Preparation
When dredging fish, seafood or chicken with flour or cornmeal to coat, prepare just before ready to cook. If the food stands with its coating for too long before cooking, the coating will become soggy.

Variation
If desired, the trout may be dredged with plain or whole-wheat flour instead of the cornmeal.

SERVES 2

SWEET-SOUR FISH

In China this dish is almost always
prepared with freshwater fish, but
sea bass is also an excellent choice.

1 sea bass, gray mullet or carp, weighing about 2lbs,
 cleaned
1 tbsp dry sherry
Few slices fresh ginger
½ cup sugar
6 tbsps cider vinegar
1 tbsp soy sauce
2 tbsps cornstarch
1 clove garlic, crushed
2 green onions, shredded
1 small carrot, peeled and finely shredded
1oz bamboo shoots, shredded

1. Rinse the fish well inside and out. Make three diagonal
cuts on each side of the fish with a sharp knife.

2. Trim off the fins, leaving the dorsal fin on top.

3. Trim the tail to two neat points.

4. Bring enough water to cover the fish to the boil in a wok.
Gently lower the fish into the boiling water and add the
sherry and ginger. Cover the wok tightly and remove at
once from the heat. Allow to stand 15-20 minutes to let the
fish cook in the residual heat.

5. To test if the fish is cooked, pull the dorsal fin – if it comes
off easily the fish is done. If not, return the wok to the heat
and bring to the boil. Remove from the heat and leave the
fish to stand a further 5 minutes. Transfer the fish to a heated
serving dish and keep it warm. Take all but 4 tbsps of the fish
cooking liquid from the wok. Add the remaining ingredients
including the vegetables and cook, stirring constantly, until
the sauce thickens. Spoon some of the sauce over the fish
to serve and serve the rest separately.

Step 1 Rinse the
fish well and
make three
diagonal cuts on
each side.

Step 2 Using
kitchen scissors,
trim all of the fins
except the dorsal
fin at the top.

Step 3 Using
kitchen scissors
again, trim the
ends of the tail to
two sharp points.

 *Cook's Notes*

 Time
Preparation takes about 25
minutes, cooking takes about
15-25 minutes.

 Cook's Tip
The diagonal cuts in the side
of the fish ensure even
cooking.

 Variation
If desired, use smaller fish
such as trout or red mullet and
shorten the cooking time to 10-15
minutes.

Preparation
The fish may also be cooked
in the oven in a large roasting
pan or in greased foil sprinkled with
sherry. Cook at 375°F for 10 minutes
per ½ inch thickness, measured
around the middle of the fish.

SERVES 4-6

STUFFED FISH

A whole baked fish makes an impressive main course for a dinner party. The stuffing makes the fish go further and with no bones it's easy to serve and eat.

2-3lb whole fish such as carp, sea bass or salmon trout
2 tbsps melted butter

Stuffing

1 tbsp butter or margarine
1 small onion, finely chopped
4oz mushrooms, roughly chopped
1 hard-cooked egg, peeled and roughly chopped
¾ cup fresh breadcrumbs, white or whole-wheat
Pinch salt and pepper
2 tsps chopped fresh dill
2 tsps chopped fresh parsley
Pinch nutmeg

Sauce

½ cup sour cream
Pinch sugar
Granted rind and juice of ½ lemon
Pinch salt and white pepper
Lemon slices and parsley sprigs to garnish

1. Ask the fishmonger to gut and bone the fish for you, leaving on the head and tail. Sprinkle the cavity of the fish with salt and pepper and set it aside while preparing the stuffing.

2. To chop the onion finely, peel it and cut it in half lengthwise. Place the onion cut side down on a chopping board. Using a large, sharp knife, make four cuts into the onion, parallel to the chopping board, but not completely through to the root end. Using the pointed tip of the knife, make four or five cuts into the onion lengthwise, following the nat-

Step 2 Slice the onion crosswise into individual dice.

ural lines in the onion and not cutting through to the root end. Next, cut the onion crossways into thin or thick slices as desired and the onion should fall apart into individual dice. Keep fingers well out of the way when slicing.

3. Melt the butter or margarine in a medium-sized saucepan and add the chopped onion and mushrooms. Cook briefly to soften the vegetables and set aside. Stir in the remaining stuffing ingredients.

4. Spread the stuffing evenly into the cavity of the fish and place the fish in lightly buttered foil or in a large baking dish. Sprinkle the top with melted butter and bake in a preheated 350°F oven for about 40 minutes, basting frequently. If the fish begins to dry out too much on top, cover loosely with aluminum foil.

5. When the fish is cooked, combine the sauce ingredients and pour over the fish. Cook a further 5 minutes to heat the sauce, but do not allow it to bubble. Remove the fish to a serving dish and garnish with lemon and parsley.

Cook's Notes

Cook's Tip
Cover the head and tail of the fish with lightly greased foil about halfway through cooking time. This will prevent the fish from drying out and improve the appearance of the finished dish.

Time
Preparation takes about 20 minutes. If boning the fish yourself, add a further 30 minutes. Cooking takes approximately 45 minutes.

Variation
Other vegetables, such as grated carrot, finely chopped green or red pepper or peeled, seeded and chopped tomatoes may be added to the stuffing.

SERVES 4

POISSON EN PAPILLOTE

A famous New Orleans dish that cannot fail to
impress at a special dinner party, this recipe
demands the use of freshly prepared fish stock.

8 single or 4 double whitefish fillets
Fishbones and trimmings
1 bay leaf, sprig thyme and 2 parsley stalks
6 black peppercorns
1 slice lemon
1 cup dry white wine
1 cup water
8 large uncooked shrimp, shelled
4 crab claws, cracked and shelled
¼ cup butter or margarine
3 tbsps flour
1 onion, finely chopped
Pinch salt and pepper
2 egg yolks

1. Preheat the oven to 400°F. To make fish stock, skin the fish fillets and place the skin in a large stockpot along with the fish bones, thyme, bay leaf, peppercorns and lemon slice. Add the wine and water and bring to the boil. Lower the heat and simmer for 20 minutes. Strain and set aside.

2. Cut wax paper or baking parchment into large ovals big enough to form a parcel for each fish fillet. Fold the paper in half and lightly oil both sides.

3. Place the fish fillets on one half of the paper and arrange the shrimp and crab claws on top of each fillet.

4. Melt the butter in a heavy-based saucepan and, when foaming, add the flour. Cook over moderate heat for 2-3 minutes, stirring frequently until a pale straw color. Add the onion and cook until lightly browned.

5. Gradually pour on the fish stock, whisking continuously. Cook over moderate heat for about 4-5 minutes, or until the

Step 3 Place the fish fillets, shrimp and crab claws on the greased paper.

Step 6 Spoon the prepared sauce over the fish.

sauce thickens.

6. Mix the egg yolks with a few spoonfuls of the hot sauce and then stir the egg yolks into the sauce. Spoon some of the sauce over each fillet and seal the parcels, folding the edge over twice and twisting the ends slightly to seal completely.

7. Place the parcels on baking sheets or in shallow baking pans and place in the preheated oven for about 20 minutes.

8. Serve the parcels unopened, to be opened at the table. Serve any remaining sauce separately.

Cook's Notes

Time
Preparation takes about 40 minutes. Cooking takes about 20 minutes for the stock, 7-8 minutes for the sauce and 20 minutes to finish the dish.

Cook's Tip
When making fish stock, cook for only 20 minutes with the fishbones in. Overcooking will result in a bitter tasting stock.

Preparation
If reheating extra sauce to serve, place over gentle heat and stir constantly until heated through. Do not allow the sauce to boil or the sauce will curdle.

INDEX